Clarke Quay and Boat Quay · Here you'll find some of the hottest restaurants and clubs in town *(page 30)*

Pulau Ubin · Escape from the urban jungle to this rustic island *(page 78)*

Sentosa Island · Touristy it may be, but Sentosa has some of Singapore's best beaches and historical sights *(page 73)*

Night Safari · The best afterdark activity *(page 71)*

Little India · Get pleasantly lost in its colourful backstreets *(page 50)*

The National Museum · There's more than just history on offer here – check out its handsome interiors too *(page 37)*

CONTENTS

■ **Introduction** 7

■ **A Brief History** 14

■ **Where to Go** 25

A ➤ in the text denotes a highly recommended sight

Singapore River 25

North Bank 25, South Bank 27, Marina Bay 27, Boat Quay and Upriver 29

Civic District 31

City Hall 31, Armenian Street 34, Fort Canning Park 35, National Museum 37, Art Museum 37, CHIJMES 38, The Raffles 39

Chinatown 41

Chinatown Heritage Centre 42, Chinatown Streets 43, Tanjong Pagar District 45, Singapore City Gallery 46, Club Street 47, Telok Ayer Street 48, Thian Hock Keng Temple 49, Art and Design 49

Little India 50

Serangoon Road 50, Sri Veeramakaliamman Temple 51, Sri Srinivasa Perumal Temple 52, Buddhist Temples 53

Kampong Glam 54

Arab Street 54, Sultan Mosque 55, Malay Heritage Centre 55, Kampong Glam Shopping 55, More Historic Mosques 56, Bugis 57, Waterloo Street 58

Orchard Road 59

60

26

76

Geylang Serai and Katong 61

Zoos, Parks and Orchid Gardens 62

*Singapore Botanic Gardens 62, Chinese and
Japanese Gardens 63, Haw Par Villa 64,
Jurong BirdPark 66, Bukit Timah Nature Reserve
67, MacRitchie Reservoir Park 68, Mandai Orchid
Gardens 69, Singapore Zoo 69, Night Safari 71*

Island Excursions 73

Sentosa 73, Southern Islands 77, Pulau Ubin 78

What to Do 81

Eating Out 98

Handy Travel Tips 106

Hotels and Restaurants 128

Index 143

Features

Singapore Tidbits 8
It Pays to be a Politician 21
Historical Landmarks 23
Bay Buzz 28
Preservation and Destruction 32
Love Potions 42
The Feather in Singapore's Cap 66
Wartime Memories 72
Chek Jawa 78
Money-Back Guarantees 83
Complaints Departments 87
Calendar of Events 97
Tea with the Queen 102
Cookery Schools 105

INTRODUCTION

Singapore is a very small island nation with very large attractions and achievements. Strategically situated on the tip of the Malaysian peninsula between the Indian Ocean and the South China Sea, Singapore has made itself the busiest port in the world, the second-largest oil refiner on the planet and a major international financial centre. While Singapore's astonishing wealth sets it apart from most tiny islands, it is its population that makes it unique. A melding of Chinese, Malay and Indian peoples, this Southeast Asian crossroads has become a model of ethnic and religious tolerance. While the different ethnic groups continue to celebrate their own cultural heritage, it is not uncommon to see the comfortable intermingling of races. A Malay wedding, for instance, can take place right next to a Chinese funeral at a void deck, which is the ground floor of a public housing apartment block. Take a walk around the city, and it's not unusual to see a Buddhist temple, a Hindu shrine and a mosque all lined up within two blocks of one another. With policies, laws and practices in place, as well as an innate tolerance and respect among the people of one another's faith and culture, Singapore is probably one of the most racially harmonious countries in the world. Singapore also stands out as the cleanest, most efficient and most highly organised society in Asia.

Yet what attracts travellers is not Singapore's wealth or its social wisdom; it is the shopping, the eating and the ethnic neighbourhoods. Shopping and eating are Singaporeans' main activities and it isn't long before visitors are swept up in these tides of delightful consumerism. Because of its special location and status as a free-trade zone, Singapore boasts good shopping

The Merlion is Singapore's tourism icon

for clothing, crafts, jewellery and goods manufactured in nearby Malaysia, Thailand and other handicraft centres of Southeast Asia. Again, because of its location, Singapore offers the most diverse culinary experience of any Asian nation. Here, the very best Chinese, Indian, Malay and an array of other international dishes are available, usually at rock-bottom prices.

Finally, for the sightseer and cultural explorer, Singapore offers historic districts to explore, from Arab Street and Little India to the Civic District and Chinatown. There are world-class modern attractions as well, from orchid gardens to the world's finest zoos. These treasures are themselves tiny but brilliant isles in an urban sea of modern shopping centres (including one with the world's largest fountain), government housing apartment blocks (home to millions of residents) and skyscrapers (where the money is counted).

It is curious how so much (culturally, ethnically and economically) is contained in so small a space. The main island of Singapore, together with over 63 surrounding islets, covers

Singapore Tidbits

- The Port of Singapore is the world's busiest port.
- Singapore supports more plant species than all of North America.
- Singaporeans' most popular leisure activity is watching TV.
- The best math students in the world attend Singapore schools.
- The Singapore Sling is still served at the place it was invented almost a century ago, the Long Bar at the Raffles Hotel.
- Most Singaporeans (more than 83 percent) live in high-rise apartments built by the government.
- The Suntec City mall contains the world's largest fountain.
- The lowest temperature ever recorded was 19.4°C (68.9°F).
- Over 90 percent of Singaporeans own mobile phones.
- The number of yearly visitors is more than twice the total population.

Soccer players at the Padang

about 699 sq km (270 sq miles) – four times smaller than Luxembourg or Rhode Island, the smallest state in the United States. Yet about half of this land consists of forest reserves, marshes and other green areas.

Green Spaces

Singapore's green zones surprise many first-time visitors, at least those expecting to find a colossal air-conditioned city-state of glass and steel housed under a plastic bubble. While crowded and expanding, with a population of 4.7 million, Singapore is not the sprawling patchwork of overlapping suburbs and housing developments one encounters in such large modern cities as Los Angeles. Instead, Singapore can be said to be a vertical Los Angeles. More than 83 percent of its residents live in housing estates that consist of neatly kept apartment towers stretching to the sky. These residential towers are distributed across the main island in suburban

Chingay street parade entertainers

towns, many of which have their own subway stations, shopping malls, libraries, community centres and other urban services. Within the tower clusters and between the towns, there are extensive green zones and areas of parkland.

Although linked to Malaysia by geography and by history, Singapore is an independent country, with a population dominated by Chinese (76 percent). Malays make up 14 percent of Singapore's citizens, Indians 8 percent, with the remaining 2 percent comprising Eurasians, Arabs, Jews and other minority groups. There are four official languages (English, Malay, Mandarin Chinese and Tamil), with English designated as the language of administration and Malay as the national language. But on the ground, many Singaporeans also speak Singlish, a colloquial language that involves a mix of English, Chinese dialects and Malay. Most Chinese speak a variety of languages, such Hokkien, Teochew and Cantonese, reflecting the various origins of Singaporean Chinese.

One ethnic group that has played a large part in shaping the customs, architecture and cuisine of Singapore are the Straits Chinese or Peranakan, a hybrid race that evolved from intermarriage between Chinese migrants from mainland China and native Malays. The men are known as *baba* and the women *nyonya*, and they have a culture that is a charming blend of Malay, Chinese and British elements. The British themselves also exerted a lasting influence on the language, customs and administration, since they literally created modern Singapore in 1819 and guided its destiny until a new self-governing constitution was approved in 1959.

Wired for Success

Singapore is a well-wired nation, with many homes linked to a countrywide network of fibre-optic cables supplying a range of services, from cable TV (80 channels) to broadband Internet. The government's goal is to turn Singapore into a truly connected city by establishing an ultra-high-speed, open and seamless network under a masterplan known as iN2015, or Intelligent Nation 2015.

Singapore's transportation system is a showcase of national industry. The subway (MRT) serves over one million people daily and continues to expand to all corners of the main island. Over 20,000 taxis serve the city. Cabs are inexpensive, clean and accept a variety of credit cards. Only about a third of Singapore's residents (who enjoy the second-highest per capita income in Asia) can afford a personal car due to the deliberate imposition of high

Free WiFi

Free wireless internet access is available at many public places in Singapore under the Wireless@SG scheme. Simply register online with a service provider and using a WiFi-capable mobile device, you can surf away. *(See page 118 for details.)*

taxes, restrictions on car use and tariffs levied on automobile ownership. This, along with other tough traffic regulations, has kept the downtown area from experiencing the gridlock and road rage common to other metropolitan areas. Singapore's airport, often hailed as the best in the world, enjoys the same unrestricted flow; clearing customs and immigration is often a matter of how fast you can walk.

Of course, Singapore's efficiency, orderliness, cleanliness and general good behaviour has come at what some critics consider a steep price. Even locals joke that Singapore is a 'fine' country, seeing as how the government has imposed a fine on nearly every objectionable behaviour, from not flushing public toilets to selling chewing gum. Singapore is also known as a country with severe penalties for more serious offences. Caning is prescribed for some crimes; the death penalty is always enforced for drug smuggling. But what some Westerners perceive as an authoritarian city-state, with draconian laws and little personal freedom, is regarded by many Singaporeans as merely the common-sense way to run society. Singapore's economic success and its ability to combat such social ills as drug use, corruption and pollution have made it the envy of many emerging nations and a model for Asia in general.

For sceptical Westerners, seeing Singapore for themselves can be an eye-opener. This is certainly not an oppressed population. On the contrary, Singaporeans tend to be outgoing and cheerful, if a little competitive and aggressive. Some say that social engineering in Singapore has proved a success because it is built on the traditional Confucian and Asian values of the region. While Singa-

Respecting elders

In Singapore respect is shown to one's elders; children are legally obliged to support their parents during retirement years.

pore is cosmopolitan and Western in outlook, it is at the core a society of people who place a high value on family and nation, racial tolerance and consensus.

While a few visitors might judge the politics of Singapore as oppressive, everyone could be forgiven for finding the weather so. Just 136 km (85 miles) north of the equator, Singapore is hot and humid all year round. It hardly cools off at night by more than a few degrees. The lowest temperature ever recorded in Singapore was a 'chilly' 19.4°C (68.9°F). The high humidity leaves most visitors drenched in sweat short-

A cosmopolitan country

ly after hitting the streets. Fortunately, ever ingenious Singapore has taken on the forces of the climate, too. In public areas, everything that can be air-conditioned usually is, from buses to shopping malls.

Instant Asia

For some, Singapore is a welcome stopover, its top-rated airport making it the perfect gateway to Thailand, Indonesia, Malaysia, Cambodia and Vietnam. For others, Singapore, with its legendary cleanliness and hygiene, its widespread use of English and its celebrated sights, shops and ethnic eateries, is a significant destination in its own right – an ideal introduction, in fact, to all of Asia.

A BRIEF HISTORY

With its location at the crossroads of Southeast Asia's sea lanes, it's no surprise that Singapore has long functioned as a major trading post. Malay, Indian and Chinese merchants plied the Straits of Malacca for centuries; Chinese sailors apparently named the island Pu-luo-chung (Island at Land's End) as early as the 3rd century AD. Malays settled on the island by the 7th century, naming it Temasek (Sea Town), and Marco Polo may have sailed by it in the late 13th century. Around the 14th century, the Sumatran prince Sang Nila Utama, seeking shelter on the island from a storm, gave it its modern name after sighting what he thought was a lion. More likely he saw a tiger, native to Singapore and Malaysia. The name 'Singapura' is Sanskrit for 'Lion City', and Singapore has been the Lion City ever since, regardless of the fact that no wild lions ever roamed here.

Pirates used the island as a base for centuries, and control of Singapore, the Malay peninsula and the Straits of Malacca wavered between Siamese and East Javan conquerors until the arrival of Raffles, the founder of modern Singapore.

Raffles Rules

Sir Thomas Stamford Raffles (1781–1826) only visited Singapore briefly over a four-year period, but he left a giant's imprint on the island. An officer of the British East India Company and a colonial entrepreneur of extraordinary vision, Raffles spoke the Malay language and knew its customs. He governed Java and wrote a history of the region, but his goal was to establish a trading post in strategic waters between Indonesia and Malaysia, where the Dutch, as well as the British, had considerable colonial holdings. Raffles succeeded in this aim when he landed on the banks of the Singapore River on

Singapore in 1870 – junks with Fort Canning Hill behind

29 January 1819 and signed treaties with contending Malay sultans, thus establishing Singapore as a British trading post. The Dutch recognised the claim in 1824. In 1826, Malacca, Penang and Singapore effectively became British trading colonies under the British Straits Settlements.

Upon his arrival in 1819, Raffles found an island shrouded in dense jungle and swamp, occupied by a few Malay families and some Chinese traders. Free-trade policies and firm but liberal colonial rule under Raffles' direction soon created a boomtown of 10,000 residents, where 2,000 ships called annually. The sultans sold Singapore's rights to the British in 1824 and Raffles continued his social reforms (abolishing slavery), cleared the land and oversaw an ambitious construction campaign. He opened Singapore to immigration, bringing in labourers, merchants and businessmen from all over Southeast Asia and most notably from China. Raffles, in short, laid the groundwork for the vibrant free port of Singapore that remains in place today.

Raffles arrived in 1819

Raffles created colonial Singapore in astonishingly short order. On his first visit in 1819 he stayed only one week, placing Colonel William Farquhar in command. He returned the same year for three weeks, devising the familiar outlines of the city, with its Colonial District on the Singapore River. When Raffles next visited three years later, he relieved Farquhar of command and oversaw the final details of Singapore's reconstruction. By the time Raffles left Singapore for the last time, in June 1823, he had laid the cornerstone for a college that united Malay and European students in East–West studies. The following year, a ship fire destroyed all his writings about the region and his extensive natural history specimens. He died without heir in London in 1826, a day short of his 45th birthday.

Rubber and Tin

The British success in Singapore depended on many elements, including cooperation with the Chinese clan organisations (the *kongsi*) and complicity in the opium trade, which was a major source of revenue from the 1830s onwards. Singapore became a British colony officially in 1867, just before the opening of the Suez Canal in 1869, which further spurred trade in the Straits of Malacca. In the first 50 years after Raffles' appearance, the island's population mushroomed from a few hundred to over 100,000. As the 20th century loomed, the export of rubber and tin became Singapore's major industry. The pirate coves and tiger dens of earlier times were erased; rubber plantations and tin mines ruled the region.

Generations of Chinese migrants from China, many of whom married locals, came to be ardent supporters of British ways. These Straits Chinese dominated local politics and formed the wealthier ranks of the mercantile class under colonial rule, but they kept in touch with the Chinese mainland as well. Sun Yat Sen arrived in Singapore to set up a branch of his revolutionary party in 1906.

The Great Depression in the West swept through Singapore in 1929, hurling many miners and rubber tappers into extreme poverty, but the 1920s also saw the ascent of Singapore millionaires, including Aw Boon Haw, the purveyor of the Tiger Balm ointment. Discontent with colonial rule increased in the 1930s, alongside the rise of India's independence movement and China's Communist Party. The revolution was, however, put on hold by World War II.

Street hawkers, 1924

The Fall of Singapore

Winston Churchill would call the fall of Singapore to the Japanese in 1942 'the worst disaster and the largest capitulation' in English history. The British, confident of an attack from the sea, had built a strong naval defense in Singapore and

General Percival led the surrender of British troops in 1942

armed Sentosa Island to the south with large guns, but the Japanese came overland, sweeping down the Malay peninsula on foot and by bicycle, eventually seizing nearby Johor Bahru. Outnumbered three to one, the Japanese nevertheless struck quickly after landing in Singapore, occupying Bukit Timah, which held the British food and fuel depots, and bluffed the British into surrender in seven days. Nearly 30,000 prisoners of war were incarcerated in Changi Prison, near the present airport. They were later led on a forced march through Malaysia all the way to Thailand, where many died building the railway and bridge over the River Kwai.

Residents of Singapore, especially those of Chinese ancestry, were punished more severely than the Australian, Indian and British soldiers, since they had opposed Japan's earlier occupation of China. By the time of Japan's surrender in 1945, about 100,000 Singapore residents had died by execution or of starvation.

The British resumed control after World War II, but their authority was now much diminished and Singapore's desire for political autonomy was strong. The British slowly relaxed their control in the region, creating a Federation of Malaya and also making Singapore – which was predominately Chinese – a separate Crown Colony in 1955. The colony's first chief minister, David Marshall, demanded independence, but Britain would not agree. In the meantime, a new party was rising in Singapore, headed by a new leader who would shape a modern Singapore as profoundly as Raffles had shaped the colonial city-state.

Lee Kuan Yew in Charge

Singapore's modern-day Raffles was Lee Kuan Yew. Lee, born in 1923 to Straits Chinese parents, graduated from the University of Cambridge with honours. Returning to Singapore in 1950, he cast his lot with those advocating the overthrow of the British, helping to form the People's Action Party (PAP) in 1955. Supporting labour unions, working with local communists and calling for a merger with the rest of Malaya, the PAP won the first internal self-government elections of 1959 and Lee became Singapore's prime minister.

Then, quickly cutting his links with the communist and leftist elements, Lee concentrated on severing ties with Britain by uniting with Malaya, Sabah and Sarawak to create the Federation of Malaysia in 1963.

It was not long, however, before Singapore was being viewed as a threat to the new Malaysian republic. Muslim

Singapore story

For an insight into Singapore's meteoric rise, read *The Singapore Story*, the vivid and fascinating memoirs of Singapore's first prime minister Lee Kuan Yew, who has deservedly been credited with bringing the country to where it is today.

Lee Kuan Yew in 1967

forces hastened the expulsion of Singapore, which came in 1965, dashing Lee's dream of Malaysian unity after just 23 months, but leading directly to Singapore's full independence.

Many doubted whether Singapore had the resources, the will and the genius to survive as a tiny independent nation, but Lee seemed to supply all three elements. As prime minister from 1959 to 1990, Lee has been hailed, especially in Singapore itself, as the singular architect of his nation. He harmonised the contending ethnic forces, brought strict order to society, emphasised efficiency, embraced Western ideas, dealt harshly with his political opponents, ruled the nation like a father and focused unrelentingly on economic progress. So far, his People's Action Party has not spent a single day out of office since independence, and most Singaporeans venerate Lee Kuan Yew as the country's founding father.

The New Singapore

Under Lee Kuan Yew and his successors, Goh Chok Tong and Lee Hsien Loong, Singapore has continued to be one of Southeast Asia's brightest stars over the last three decades. The government's paternal approach has defused racial and labour disputes, public housing schemes have provided most citizens with their own homes, and trade and business policies have attracted plenty of foreign trade and investment. While Singapore's massive modernisation has its critics and much of old Singapore has been razed, the standard of living has risen to the highest international benchmarks. Social engineering projects – which include banning smoking in public places, outlawing the sale of chewing gum, monitoring public toilets for flushing, imposing huge taxes on car ownership and running state-sponsored matchmaking services – have drawn sneers from overseas, but Singapore is the most mannerly and cleanest of all Asian cities.

From the perspective of Western democracies, Singapore's great achievements have come at the expense of personal and political freedom. Dissidents have been jailed or exiled, and critical publications have been banned (*Asian Wall Street Journal*, 1985) or sued (*International Herald Tribune*, 1994) for unflattering coverage. The local media, from TV to newspapers, have often censored themselves into blandness. The case of David Marshall (1908–1995), one of Singapore's founding fathers, is illustrative. A Singapore-born Jew whose parents were from Iraq, Marshall was educated in Britain,

It Pays to be a Politician

Singapore's politicians are among the highest paid in the world. The president draws a high annual pay (also known as the Privy Purse) of more than S$3.8 million (US$2.8 million), on top of a yearly entertainment allowance of some S$130,000 (US$85,000). Just as attractive is the prime minister's annual salary of just over S$3.7 million (US$2.7 million) while a junior cabinet minister gets a pay of S$1.9 million (US$1.4 million) a year. Comparatively the President of the United States pulls in only US$400,000 annually.

The government believes that high salaries are necessary to attract the best talents and to prevent corruption. And because political leaders are expected to perform like CEOs, they should be paid like corporate honchos. The salaries of Singapore's ministers are determined by benchmarking to those of top earners in six professions.

became a prisoner of war when the Japanese invaded Singapore, and later established himself as Singapore's best criminal defense attorney. He was elected as Singapore's first chief minister in 1955 but, with the rise of Lee Kuan Yew and the PAP, soon found himself cast in the role of dissenter. In 1969, Lee and his government banned all trials by jury, putting a severe dent in Marshall's high-profile career. Marshall was among the very few in Singapore to openly oppose caning as a punishment for minor criminal offences. The year before his death he branded Lee a fascist.

Such a view in Singapore today is perhaps that of the minority. Full employment, bureaucratic efficiency, social stability and a continued high standard of living have pleased most residents, who are free to vote out the ruling party under Singapore's parliamentary system. The ruling party has promised to open the political process to the people and, by making Singapore a more cultured society, stem the brain drain of some of its most highly educated citizens to the West. How Singapore will shape itself to meet raised expectations in the 21st century remains an open question, one that may take the rise of another Stamford Raffles or Lee Kuan Yew to answer.

Most Singaporeans live in public housing

Historical Landmarks

14th century Singapura (Sanskrit for 'Lion City') is named by Sang Nila Utama, a Sumatran prince.

15th century Singapore is made part of the Malay kingdom of Melaka.

1819 Sir Stamford Raffles makes Singapore a British trading post.

1824 Singapore is purchased by the British East India Company.

1826 Singapore is administered by the East India Company as part of the Straits Settlements together with Melaka and Penang.

1867 The Straits Settlements become a British Crown Colony.

1869 Suez Canal opens and Singapore becomes an important stop along the main shipping route for rubber.

1942 Singapore is occupied by the Japanese army.

1945 The Japanese occupation ends.

1946 The British make Singapore a Crown Colony.

1955 David Marshall heads the first elected government.

1959 Singapore achieves self-government; Lee Kuan Yew and the People's Action Party (PAP) control the new parliament.

1963 Singapore joins the Federation of Malaysia.

1965 Singapore separates from Malaysia and becomes an independent state. Lee Kuan Yew heads the new Republic of Singapore.

1990 Goh Chok Tong takes over from Lee Kuan Yew, who continues to serve as a powerful senior minister.

1998 The economy is affected by the Asian financial crisis.

1999 The economy makes a dramatic turnaround.

2003 The SARS outbreak is efficiently brought under control.

2004 Lee Hsien Loong takes over as prime minister. Goh Chok Tong continues as senior minister and Lee Kuan Yew, minister mentor.

2005 The green light is given to legalise casino gambling and the building of two 'integrated resorts', mega entertainment and leisure complexes, at Marina Bay and Sentosa. SR Nathan returns for his second term as president.

2006 The PAP wins 82 of 84 seats in the general elections.

2008 Singapore wins bid to host inaugural Youth Olympic Games.

WHERE TO GO

Singapore can take days to explore. In addition to excellent eating and shopping, there are plenty of attractions well worth taking in. The leading sights are grouped here by district, with most located near the heart of the city and the Singapore River, which flows through it. Many of the older neighbourhoods and attractions have been modernised, but there are also some areas that have escaped renewal and offer a window on to old Singapore.

SINGAPORE RIVER

A good place to begin exploration is the **Singapore River**. This was where Sir Thomas Stamford Raffles, Singapore's founder, and early traders and immigrants first landed. The mangrove swamps, sultans' palaces and floating skulls deposited by pirates are long gone, as are the junks and coolies. The river, now cleaned up, is lined by conservation shophouses painted in colourful hues and surrounded by colonial architectural gems.

North Bank

Raffles' Landing Site on the north bank of the river is where Sir Stamford Raffles first landed in 1819. The spot is marked by a white marble statue cast in 1972 from a bronze one that is a stone's throw away in front of the Victoria Theatre. Flanking the white statue is the **Asian Civilisations Museum** (1 Empress Place; open Mon 1–7pm, Tues–Thur and Sat–Sun 9am–7pm, Fri 9am–9pm; admission fee; tel: 6332 2982; <www.acm.org.sg>). Built as government offices in 1865, the stately neoclassical building now showcases an excellent

School children on a field trip to Raffles' Landing Site

The Singapore River runs past the Central Business District

collection of artefacts documenting the civilisations of East, Southeast, South and West Asia. You can easily spend half a day viewing the well-curated displays here. The river-facing side of the building, **Empress Place Waterfront**, has trendy restaurants and bars.

Next to the museum is another ensemble of magnificent colonial architecture. The **Victoria Theatre** (9 Empress Place; tel: 6338 8283) and **Concert Hall** (11 Empress Place; tel: 6338 4401) were Singapore's old Town Hall and Queen Victoria Memorial Hall. The original bronze statue of Sir Stamford Raffles, which dates back to 1887, stands in front of the two buildings. Just behind is **The Arts House** (1 Old Parliament Lane; tel: 6332 6900; <www.theartshouse.com. sg>), built in 1827 as Singapore's courthouse and serving as the Parliament House from 1965 to 1999. It now has a 200-seat chamber staging arts performances, a visual arts gallery and a 75-seat art-house cinema.

South Bank

From Empress Place Waterfront extends **Cavenagh Bridge**, built of iron rails from Scotland in 1869 to connect the financial and administrative districts that Raffles had envisioned. This pedestrian bridge leads to the skyscrapers of **Raffles Place**, the heart of Singapore's **Central Business District** (CBD) that defines modern Singapore's skyline. A handful of grand neo-Renaissance bank and office buildings remain, dwarfed by modern giants of finance such as UOB Plaza, OUB Centre and Republic Plaza (three of Singapore's tallest buildings, all attaining the maximum permitted height of 280m (918ft), or about 66 storeys). Singapore's financial towers have been designed by international architects such as I.M. Pei, always in accordance with traditional Chinese principles of *feng shui*, which dictate the most propitious locations, shapes and decorative flourishes of the city's Western-style high-rises.

Next to Raffles Place is the lavish **Fullerton Hotel** (1 Fullerton Square; tel: 6733 8388; <www.fullertonhotel.com>), built as the General Post Office in 1928. The hotel, with grand columns outside and a contemporary interior, stands on the site of Fort Fullerton, which guarded the entrance to Singapore from 1829 to 1873. The hotel's Post Bar is a firm favourite with the well-heeled.

Marina Bay

An underpass below the Fullerton emerges at **One Fullerton**, a waterfront dining and nightlife hub. At the north end of One Fullerton is the **Merlion Park**, where

River sculpture

A handful of public sculptures dot the Singapore River area. Of note are Fernando Botero's *Bird* and Salvador Dali's *Homage to Newton* outside and at the foyer of UOB Plaza respectively. There are also bronze sculptures depicting life along the river in the early days.

the Merlion statue – the city's iconic mascot with the head of a lion and the body of a fish. This 8-m (26-ft)-high sculpture was commissioned in 1972 by the Singapore Tourism Board as a welcome figure to visitors. It is *de rigueur* to come here to snap a picture of the Merlion against the gleaming city skyline.

Across the water is **Esplanade – Theatres on the Bay** (1 Esplanade Drive; tel: 6828 8377; <www.esplanade.com>), the epicentre of Singapore's arts scene. Its unique architecture, resembling the husk of the thorny durian fruit Singaporeans love to eat, has been much debated. Inside are a 1,600-seat concert hall and a 2,000-seat theatre – both with exceptional acoustics. Local and international artists and groups perform year round while the shops and restaurants, notably My Humble House and Space@Humble House *(see page 136)*, are reasons enough to linger.

You can take a **bumboat**, or river taxi (tel: 6336 6111; <www.rivercruise.com.sg>), from any of the jetties near Raffles' Landing Site, Merlion Park, Boat Quay, the Esplanade and Clarke Quay for a narrated tour.

Bay Buzz

No urban planning initiative in Singapore has generated as much buzz as the new Marina Bay development <www.marina-bay.sg>. The vision for it is as thrilling as it is ambitious. Set to be completed by 2010, it will be anchored by the S$5-billion Marina Bay Sands, touted as the most expensive ever built by the American casino-resort giant Las Vegas Sands. The lavish resort will include Singapore's first-ever casino, two 2,000-seat theatres, three luxury hotel towers, conference facilities, restaurants run by celebrity chefs and an art and science museum. Complementing the resort are a financial centre, water sports venue, luxury housing and lush tropical gardens.

A bumboat ride offers an excellent view of the city skyline as the boat chugs into **Marina Bay**, an inner harbour created by massive land reclamation projects that include Collyer Quay and Clifford Pier to the south, and the area to the north where the Esplanade and **Suntec City** stand. Suntec City is a business, convention and shopping complex known for its colossal **Fountain of Wealth**. The bumboat will circle around the bay, giving you a glimpse of the world's busiest port where supertankers and container ships anchor as far out as the horizon. Development of the Marina Bay waterfront

The distinctive Esplanade – Theatres on the Bay

into a premier business and leisure area is under way; this includes the 165-m (540-ft)-high **Singapore Flyer** observation wheel, (30 Raffles Avenue; open daily 8.30am–10.30pm; admission fee; tel: 6333 3311; <www.singaporeflyer.com>), which opened in 2008, and the Marina Bay Sands (*see left*).

Boat Quay and Upriver

Raffles originally ordered the creation of five embankments along the Singapore River by reclamation. Collyer Quay and Raffles Quay were built south of the river's mouth; Boat Quay, Clarke Quay and Robertson Quay lined the river inland through the heart of the city.

Boat Quay is a great dining and drinking venue

Boat Quay runs on the southwest side of the river between the Cavenagh Bridge and Elgin Bridge. Completed in 1929 to connect the Chinese and Indian communities, it was a landfill project that handled most of Singapore's trade then. The river's commercial traffic is now gone, but Boat Quay is enjoying a second lease of life with restaurants and drinking holes in its conservation shophouses, popular with tourists and executives from the nearby Raffles Place *(see page 90)*.

Upriver from Boat Quay, on the north bank, is **Clarke Quay**, the site of scores of 19th-century godowns built by colonialists and Chinese merchants. Several of the latter became millionaires through their trading businesses at Clarke Quay. The old godowns have been restored into trendy shops peddling a host of merchandise and services, restaurants and pubs *(see pages 90–1)*.

Most tourists don't usually venture as far as **Robertson Quay**, a little further upriver, but it is a pleasant shoreline walk from Clarke and Boat quays. This former warehouse area is the largest of the three quays and is pleasantly uncrowded. The **Singapore Tyler Print Institute** (41 Robertson Quay; open Tues–Sat 10am–6pm; free; tel: 6336 3663; <www.stpi.com.sg>) houses a fine collection of printed works, a printmaking workshop and a paper mill. In the vicinity as well are good restaurants and cafés, the **Singapore Repertory Theatre** (20 Merbau Road; tel: 6221 5585; <www.srt.com.sg>) and the avant-garde boutique **Gallery Hotel** (1 Nanson Road; tel: 6849 8686; <www.galleryhotel.com.sg>).

CIVIC DISTRICT

For decades, visitors to downtown Singapore have referred to the area north of the lower Singapore River as the Colonial District, and for good reason. This is where many of the colonial-era buildings and museums stand. Raffles had assigned the north side of the river for the British from the beginning, ordering the building of offices, banks, hotels, churches and clubs there. He even built his house on the top of Fort Canning Hill. The leading colonial architects of the time were George Coleman, who consulted with Raffles on many designs, and John Bidwell, who brought neo-Renaissance plans to the Raffles Hotel, the Goodwood Park Hotel, the Victoria Theatre and many other buildings. Fortunately, many of these buildings in what has been renamed the **Civic District**, roughly the area between the Dhoby Ghaut and City Hall MRT stations, have been preserved.

City Hall

Rising above the City Hall MRT Station and accessed via North Bridge Road in an expanse of greenery is the **St Andrew's Cathedral** (open Mon–Sat 9am–5pm; tel: 6337 6104). A gazetted monument, the church owes its smooth white surface to the unique plaster that was used by Indian convict labourers. Called Madras *chunam*, it was made of egg white, eggshell, lime, sugar, coconut husk and water, and it gave the building a smooth, polished finish. This is the second place of worship on the premises. The original, which was designed in Palladian style by Coleman, was twice struck by lightning and demolished in 1852. The present cathedral, in the style of an early Gothic abbey and designed by Ronald MacPherson, was consecrated in 1862. The gleaming white exterior contrasts with the dark pews inside, with sunlight gently filtering through the coloured stained-glass windows in the morning.

Preservation and Destruction

When Singapore achieved independence in 1965, the economy was in shambles. Like every developing nation, Singapore put modernisation and economic progress on the front burner; anything that stood in the way, from historic neighbourhoods to colonial architecture, was simply razed. By the 1970s, Singapore was on its way to achieving spectacular prosperity, but it had obliterated much of its past and visitors complained that it lacked character and colour.

By the 1980s, Singapore began to heed its critics. Historic temples, office buildings, Peranakan mansions, shophouses and godowns were more often spared demolition and restored with grace.

By the late 1980s, the government focused on four areas for conservation (Boat Quay, Little India, Kampong Glam and Chinatown). More areas have been added since. For some, these efforts at preservation have come too late; others felt the preservation schemes have too often been directed by commercial, rather than aesthetic, considerations. Have Singapore's conservation measures transformed the city into a Disneyesque museum, or have they rescued outstanding architectural treasures from neglect? You decide.

If you exit the church premises onto St Andrew's Road and cross Colemen Street, you will come face to face with the **City Hall** (3 St Andrew's Road), built in ornate neoclassical style in 1929. This was where the Japanese surrendered to the British in 1945 and where Lee Kuan Yew declared Singapore's independence from British rule in 1959. Its grand staircase, with a backdrop of large Greek columns, is a favourite photography spot for wedding couples today.

Parade outside City Hall

The **old Supreme Court**, built in 1939, stands next to the City Hall. It is one of Singapore's last classical edifices with Corinthian columns. It occupies the site of Hotel de L'Europe, once the city's most elegant place to stay, according to Rudyard Kipling and other travellers. The court has now moved into the shiny glass-and-steel **new Supreme Court** building (1 Supreme Court Lane) behind. There is an observation deck on the 8th floor and a gallery on level one that traces Singapore's legal history (both open daily 8.30am–6pm; free; tel: 6226 0644). The City Hall and the old Supreme Court will be converted into a national art gallery by 2012.

Across the street from these government buildings is a large field known as the **Padang** (Malay for 'field'), where Raffles planted the British flag and ordered the ground cleared. It has long been the site of cricket matches for the members-only **Singapore Cricket Club**, founded in 1852. The club building stands on one side of the Padang, where the Japanese military rounded up the entire European population of Singapore for interrogation in 1942.

Armenian Street

The **Armenian Church** (60 Hill Street; open daily 9am–6pm; tel: 6334 0141) stands at the head of Coleman Street. Built in 1835, the church is Singapore's oldest; it is also George Coleman's masterwork. Constructed using Indian convict labour, it served refugees fleeing the war between Russia and Turkey. The churchyard contains the graves of a few of Singapore's most famous Armenian residents: the Sarkies brothers, who built Raffles Hotel, and Agnes Joachim, who discovered the orchid that would be named as Singapore's national flower, the Vanda Miss Joaquim. Round the corner

The Armenian Church is Singapore's oldest

from the Armenian Church, at 39 Armenian Street, is the **Peranakan Museum** (open Mon 1–7pm, Tues–Sun 9.30am–7pm, till 9pm on Fri; admission fee; tel: 6332 7591; <www.peranakanmuseum.sg>). The Peranakans (or Straits Chinese) have a hybrid culture that evolved through intermarriage between Chinese men and Malay women in the early days.

Also along this quiet stretch is **The Substation** (tel: 6337 7535; <www.substation.org>), a centre for artistic experimentation and cutting-edge work, converted from a disused power station. It has a tiny theatre and an equally small gallery that connects to a charming garden overhung with trees. Located in the garden is **Timbre Music Bistro** (open daily 6pm–late; tel: 6338 8277), an atmospheric nook where Singapore bands and musicians take to the stage nightly.

Fort Canning Park

Forming the western boundary of the Civic District is **Fort Canning Park**, which can be accessed via Canning Rise that adjoins Armenian Street, up a flight of stairs next to MICA Building on Hill Street or via an underpass beside Park Mall shopping centre on Penang Road.

The hill, once the site of royal palaces built by Malay sultans, was known as Forbidden Hill (Bukit Larangan), for commoners were not allowed there. The ghosts of the sultans were believed to haunt the hill, the curse not broken until British Resident William Farquhar cleared the summit and erected a cannon there for defence in the early 19th century. Raffles built a bungalow on the hill in 1822, occupying it for almost a year. Until the British surrendered to the Japanese in World War II, the hill was a military command post.

Today Fort Canning Park has a well-marked trail that makes for a nice walk. Begin at the whitewashed Fort Canning Centre, formerly an army barracks, where you can get a map of the hill. The building also houses the Singapore

One of the two Gothic-style gates on Fort Canning Hill

Dance Theatre and the cookery school **at-sunrice** (tel: 6336 3307; <www.at-sunrice.com>), which has a popular 'Spice Garden Walk & Morning Gourmet' course that brings participants on a guided tour of the spice garden *(see below)*, and then back to the school for hands-on cooking and lunch.

The main attraction is the **Battle Box** (51 Canning Rise; open daily 10am–6pm; admission fee; tel: 6333 0510; <www.legendsfortcanning.com/fortcanning/battlebox.htm>). This bomb-proof bunker with 22 rooms and corridors 9m (30ft) underground was where British Lt-General Percival decided to surrender to the Japanese (15 February 1942). The bunker is equipped with wax robots and film projections to recreate the events leading to Singapore's fall.

Other attractions at Fort Canning Park include the **ASEAN Sculpture Garden**, the original **fort gate** and a replica of the 19-hectare (47-acre) **spice garden** that

Raffles established in 1822 as the 'experimental and botanical garden' of colonial Singapore. The oasis of green in front of Fort Canning Centre is a venue for arts and music events, such as the annual Ballet Under The Stars by the Singapore Dance Theatre, usually held in July.

National Museum

The **National Museum** (open daily 10am–6pm; admission fee; tel: 6332 5642; <www.nationalmuseum.sg>), at 93 Stamford Road, is housed in one of Singapore's most impressive colonial edifices. Reopened in late 2006 after a three-year renovation, it now has a second, glass-and-steel wing and a striking giant glass rotunda on which images depicting Singapore's history are projected at night. The museum has also reinvented itself as a hip space to learn about history with its interactive displays and narratives. Look out for the Singapore History Gallery with 11 national treasures, from the Singapore Stone, a rock with inscriptions dating back to the 10th century, to 14th-century Majapahit gold ornaments from Fort Canning Hill. The museum also has an interesting line-up of performing and visual arts programmes.

National Museum

Singapore Art Museum

Along Bras Basah Road is the **Singapore Art Museum** (open Mon–Sun 10am–7pm, Fri 10am–9pm; tel: 6332 3222; admission fee, Fri 6–9pm free; <www.singart. com>). The colonial structure, dating from the early 1800s, formerly housed St Joseph's Institution, a school

Pioneer artist Georgette Chen's self-portrait

set up by Catholic missionaries. The museum's permanent collection is an excellent sampling of works by Southeast Asia's leading artists. It ranks among the finest contemporary art museums in the region (past exhibitions have included works from the Guggenheim Museum in New York). Even if not for the artworks, the museum is worth visiting just to see the splendidly restored chapel and the school hall, now called the glass hall. The latter features a colourful glass sculpture by American artist Dale Chihuly.

CHIJMES

CHIJMES (tel: 6332 6277; <www.chijmes.com.sg>) – pronounced 'chimes'– is a complex of buildings within a walled enclosure, formerly the Catholic girls' school Convent of the Holy Infant Jesus, located at the corner of Victoria Street and North Bridge Road. These buildings, which may well be the most beautiful Christian architectural legacy in Singapore, have been painstakingly restored to their original neoclassical glory. The chapel, dating from 1903, is the most magnificent. Designed by Father Charles Benedict Nain, a French priest, it is medieval in design and ornamentation. It is now used as a concert hall and a wedding venue.

The 'Gate of Hope' entrance along Bras Basah Road was once where the destitute and desperate left newborn babies in hope that the convent would adopt them. Today merrymakers – and not the impoverished – enter the convent gates. CHIJMES is now a lively nightlife hub, with the Fountain Court area hosting trendy restaurants, bars and clubs *(see page 91)* as well as a handful of boutiques and handicraft shops.

Opposite CHIJMES across Victoria Street is the oldest Roman Catholic church in Singapore, the **Cathedral of the Good Shepherd** ('A' Queen Street; gates open daily 24 hours; tel: 6337 2036), built in 1846 in Renaissance style with six porticoed entrances and a high wooden ceiling.

The Raffles

Located diagonally across CHIJMES is the **Raffles Hotel** (1 Beach Road; tel: 6337 1886; <www.raffles.com>), perhaps the most famous hotel in Asia. It began as a small hotel in 1887 founded by the Armenian Sarkies brothers. The writer Joseph Conrad was among the firsts to check in, followed in

The elegant Raffles Hotel

Doorman at Raffles Hotel

1889 by Rudyard Kipling, who praised the food but not the accommodation. The Sarkies then went on an up-grading rampage, adding the Tiffin Room, Palm Court and the Billiard Room by 1902.

Monarchs, celebrities and famous writers, including Charlie Chaplin, Somerset Maugham and John Lennon, had stayed at the Raffles. But by the 1990s the hotel was suffering from neglect and decay, leading the government to declare it a national monument and provide for a massive facelift. The restoration involved years of tracking down original plans and finding skilled craftsmen to repair and recreate the original fittings.

Nearly everyone who comes to Singapore visits the Raffles. Its **Bar & Billiard Room** is probably the most romantic spot for a drink, and the courtyard is good for open-air dining. The **Raffles Hotel Museum** (open daily 10am–7pm; free) on the third floor is small but has an intriguing collection of colonial-era hotel artefacts. And while the **Long Bar** may be nothing like the atmospheric original (despite ceiling fans and peanut shells on the floor), it is still a good place to knock back a Singapore Sling, the famous gin-based cocktail that was first concocted here in the early 1900s.

Exit the Raffles Hotel onto Seah Street to a quirky find. At No. 26 is the **Mint Museum of Toys** (open daily 9.30am–6.30pm; admission fee; tel: 6339 0660; <www.emint.com>), with a nostalgic collection of rare toys from all over the world spanning over 100 years.

CHINATOWN

Sir Thomas Stamford Raffles drew the outlines of Singapore's Chinatown in 1822, just after the first boatloads of immigrants from southern China landed at the mouth of the river. The Chinese found hard-labour jobs along the river; their fresh water source was a well on Spring Street; and gangs, triads and opium dens became a way of life. **Chinatown** then, as now, occupied a large area immediately southwest of the Singapore River. The Hokkien traders settled along today's Telok Ayer and Amoy streets; the Teochew fishermen congregated near Boat Quay; and the Cantonese merchants built shophouses along Pagoda and Temple streets.

Chinese New Year bazaar in Chinatown

   North Bridge Road and Eu Tong Sen Street are the main thoroughfares through the heart of Chinatown, lined by shopping arcades like the **People's Park Complex** (Blk 32 New Market Road), which has fashion stores and old-style fabric tenants, and the **Yue Hwa Emporium** (70 Eu Tong Sen Street; open Sun–Fri 11am–9pm, Sat 11am–10pm; tel: 6538 4222) with all things Chinese, from silk to souvenirs. The latter occupies the building of the former Great Southern Hotel, once considered the grand old lady of

Chinatown. Diagonally across Yue Hwa is **Chinatown Point**, towering above the Chinatown MRT Station and a good place to shop for Chinese art and crafts.

Chinatown Heritage Centre

Begin your exploration in Pagoda Street, where the **Chinatown Heritage Centre** (No. 48; open daily 9am–8pm; tel: 6325 2878; admission fee; <www.chinatownheritage.com.sg>) is located in a conservation shophouse. It showcases the area's cultural heritage and includes a re-creation of the cramped living conditions of early residents.

Pagoda Street joins **South Bridge Road**, the traditional area for Cantonese merchants specialising in herbal medicines and gold jewellery. Flanking this road are several sights of interest to the visitor, including two sights that are not at all Chinese. The **Jamae Mosque** (218 South Bridge Road; daily 9.30am–6pm) has distinctive pagoda-like minarets rarely seen in mosque architecture. Its unique design was

Love Potions

Aphrodisiacs are something of a Singapore obsession. **Eu Yan Sang Medical Hall** (269 South Bridge Road, opposite the Sri Mariamman Temple; open Mon–Sat 8.30am–6pm; tel: 6223 6333; <www.euyansang.com.sg>) offers a selection of the best in Chinese love potions, from deer penis wine to seahorse tonic. Likewise, any other pharmacy in Chinatown worth its ginseng will stock a fertile line of sexual herbs, tonics and antlers to lift a flagging libido. Along **Arab Street**, Malay medicinal houses favour onions for prolonging sexual stamina. Indian pharmacists, relying on the Tantric traditions and the Kama Sutra, will boil asparagus and treacle in milk and ghee, spiced with liquorice. You'll find a storehouse of the ingredients used in Indian aphrodisiacs at the **Mustafa Centre** on Syed Alwi Road in Little India.

Display at the Chinatown Heritage Centre

perhaps a gesture of deference to the predominantly Chinese neighbourhood. The mosque was constructed in 1826 by Muslim Chulia immigrants who came from South India's Coromandel Coast.

Adjacent to the mosque is **Sri Mariamman Temple** (244 South Bridge Road; open daily 7am–9pm). Dedicated to goddess Mariamman, who is known for curing serious illnesses, this is Singapore's most important and oldest Hindu temple, dating from 1827. Its *gopuram* tower is decorated with figures of Hindu gods. The interior is noted for its ceiling paintings and the temple is the site for the Thimithi ceremony (October/November) during which devotees walk on burning coals.

Chinatown Streets

The best time to visit Chinatown is January/February when its streets are adorned with lights and bright-red decorations to usher in the Chinese New Year and when crowds throng its bazaar for New Year goodies. At other times, the enclave is much quieter, despite the tourism board's efforts to enliven it. One such effort has resulted in the **Chinatown Night Market** (open Sun–Thur and public holidays 5–11pm, Fri–Sat 5pm–1am) with 215 stalls lining Pagoda, Trengganu and Sago streets. A stroll down **Temple Street** takes one past plenty of Chinese souvenir shops (with lacquerware, silks, Tiger Balm ointments) to **Trengganu Street**, now an outdoor street vendors' mall but previously an opera street with theatre stages and brothels.

Trengganu Street cuts through **Smith Street**, where you will find **Chinatown Food Street** (open Mon–Thur, Sun and public holidays 5–11pm, Fri–Sat 5pm–1am), with open-air hawker stalls offering delectable local favourites. Must-tries include *char kway teow* (fried flat rice noodles) and *rojak*, which is a salad of vegetables and fruits in a sweet black sauce.

Buddha Tooth Relic Temple and Museum

Trengganu Street ends at **Sago Street**, another colourful shopping area with Chinese medical halls, rattan weavers and pastry shops. Between Sago Street and Sago Lane is the **Buddha Tooth Relic Temple** (open daily 7am–7pm; tel: 6220 0220; <www.btrts.org.sg>. Opened in May 2007 and inspired by the Tang dynasty,

the temple houses religious artworks and Buddhist texts. The temple's centrepiece is one dogged by much controversy – a sacred tooth belonging to the Buddha. Only taken out for viewing on Vesak Day and Chinese New Year, the tooth's authencity has been questioned by several Buddhist scholars.

Tanjong Pagar District

From Sago Lane, turn right and walk to the corner of Tanjong Pagar and Neil roads, where the stately **Jinriksha Station** stands. Rickshaw coolies once parked their two-wheeled vehicles here. The station, built in 1903 in the classical style, is crowned by a dome. Jinrikshas were the main means of transport in Singapore in the early 1900s before they were replaced by three-wheeled trishaws in the 1940s. The rickshaw coolies lived around the station, renting beds in tiny cubicles in Chinatown.

Tanjong Pagar started out as a Malay fishing village. In the 1830s, the land around it was turned into a nutmeg plantation. The area became a thriving commercial hub, but by the 1960s, the neighbourhood had fallen into disrepair and would have met the wrecker's ball if it hadn't been for the government's conservation drive. It soon became an archetype for how the remainder of historic Singapore would be restored. Today the **Tanjong Pagar Conservation District** has over 190 meticulously restored shophouses, in pastel hues with wooden window shutters and high-beamed ceilings, along Neil Road, Murray Terrace, Craig Road and Duxton Hill Road. Offices, restaurants and pubs now call these shophouses home.

Further down along Neil Road past Kreta Ayer Road is the once notorious **Keong Saik Road**, a red-light district that has now been gentrified. Many of the area's splendid shophouses in the Chinese Baroque architectural style have been restored and converted into boutique hotels such as the Royal Peacock and the über-cool **Hotel 1929** (No. 50; <www.hotel1929.com>), which is largely responsible for making this strip hip. Holistic centres, bars and art galleries now share space with brothels and scruffy coffeeshops.

Singapore City Gallery

Opposite the Jinriksha Station across Maxwell Road is a local favourite, **Maxwell Food Centre**, one of Singapore's oldest hawker centres. Snaking queues are a regular sight at lunchtime.

Beside the food centre across Kadayanallur Street is the URA Centre with the **Singapore City Gallery** (45 Maxwell Road; open Mon–Sat 9am–5pm; tel: 6321 8321; <www.ura.gov.sg/gallery>, whose key attraction is a massive model of the city. Spread over two storeys are exhibits, interactive displays and touch-screen terminals as well as audio-visual programmes about this efficient city.

Kadayanallur Street leads uphill to **Ann Siang Road** but not before passing **The Scarlet**, a swanky boutique hotel (33 Erskine Road; tel: 6511 3333; <www.thescarlethotel.com>). Step in, if only to gawk at the dramatic interiors and browse the adjoining speciality shops and galleries.

Streetside calligrapher in Chinatown

Club Street

Ann Siang Road adjoins **Club Street**, once home to trade associations and the haunt of letter-writers for hire. The area is filled with finely restored shophouses (as well as a few colourful unrestored specimens). Their architectural style is not entirely Chinese. The carved decorations and swinging *pintu pagar* doors are Malay in origin, the Georgian windows and art-deco touches are European, and the tiled roofs are strictly in the Chinese style. The area is now a dining and retail district with fashionable boutiques, bars and restaurants. Look out for **Asylum** (22 Ann Siang Road; tel: 6324 2289; <www.theasylum.com.sg>), a cool local design studio-cum-retail outfit selling novel items from limited-edition sneakers to experimental-music CDs. The very chic **Front Row** (5 Ann Siang Road; tel: 6224 5502) stocks men's and women's apparel from upmarket brands such as A.P.C. and the home-grown label Woods & Woods.

Far East Square's 'Fire' gate

Telok Ayer Street

Club Street rises and dips into Upper Cross Street, the location of **Far East Square**, **China Square Food Centre** and **China Square Central**, three large food and entertainment centres. Far East Square is worth a stroll for its interesting shophouses and entrance gates that represent the five elements that make up the Chinese universe.

On the east side of Far East Square is **Telok Ayer Street**, which has a cluster of national monuments, beginning with the **Fuk Tak Chi Museum** (No. 76; open daily 10am–10pm; tel: 6532 7868; free). Formerly the Fuk Tak Chi Temple, built in 1824 and dedicated to Tua Pek Kong, the Taoist God of Prosperity, the museum has a collection of 200 artefacts, including a Chinese gold belt, abacus board and even a rental expiry notice, from early Chinatown residents. A little down the street is **Ying Fo Fui Kun** (No. 98; open Mon–Fri 9am–5pm, Sat 9am–noon; free; tel: 6533 6726), a Hakka clanhouse established in 1822, with traditional Chinese architectural elements such as carved beams and pillars. Further along are three places of worship. First up is the **Nagore Durgha Shrine** (No. 140), built in 1818 by Muslims from southern India. Closed since the 1990s, the building finally reopened in 2008 as an Indian-Muslim heritage centre.

Thian Hock Keng Temple

Beside the shrine is **Telok Ayer Green**, a tiny park with shaded seats and life-sized bronze figures depicting scenes from the past. Steps away is the **Thian Hock Keng Temple**, the Temple of Heavenly Bliss (No. 158; open daily 7.30am–5.30pm; tel: 6423 4616), built between 1839 and 1842 by the first Chinese immigrants, who dedicated this elaborate shrine to their protector, Ma Chu Poh, Goddess of the Sea. It has granite pillars from southern China, blue tiles from Holland and cast-iron railings from Scotland. Although the main altar is Taoist, a rear chamber is dedicated to Guan Yin, the Buddhist Goddess of Mercy. The last temple on Telok Ayer Street is **Al-Abrar Mosque** (No. 192; open daily 11.30am–9pm), known as the Indian (or Chulia) Mosque, which opened in 1855.

Art and Design

Follow the curve of the road past the **Telok Ayer Chinese Methodist Church** on your left. Cut through Telok Ayer Park to the red dot Traffic building for a stopover at the **red dot design museum** (28 Maxwell Road; open Fri–Tues 11am–6pm, till 8pm Sat–Sun; admission fee; tel: 6327 8027). Run by the German body that presents the prestigious red dot design award, the museum exhibits sleek products from around the world. The MAAD **(Market of Artists and Designers) flea market** (first Sat and Sun of the month 11am–7pm; <www.maad.sg>) here offers original works by young artists and designers.

Worshippers at the Thian Hock Keng Temple

LITTLE INDIA

Among the first Indian settlers were 120 assistants and soldiers who sailed to Singapore in 1819 with Raffles. They first congregated in Chulia Street, the original Indian quarter. But as cattle raising expanded along the Rochor River to the north, Indians settled in an area bisected by Serangoon Road, which is now known as **Little India**. Hindus are in the majority among Indians here and Tamil Muslims are well represented, but Chinese make up almost three quarters of Little India's population. This is perhaps Singapore's most colourful downtown neighbourhood with lively backstreets and a strong ethnic flavour.

Serangoon Road

For a walking tour of Little India, start at the **Little India Arcade** (48 Serangoon Road) between Campbell Lane and Hastings Road, opposite the fresh-produce market **Tekka Centre** (665 Buffalo Road). The arcade has several shops selling saris and *cholis* (short-waisted blouses) as well as sweets, medicines, betel nuts, carvings, brassware and more. A branch of one of Singapore's most famous South Indian restaurants, the **Banana Leaf Apolo** (tel: 6297 1595), is located here.

From Little India Arcade you can wander up Serangoon Road and explore its colourful side streets. Five-foot ways, which are covered corridors that front shophouses, run along **Campbell Lane**; shops here sell woodcarvings, furniture, musical instruments and flower garlands. **Dunlop Street** has Internet cafés, backpacker inns as well as small groceries. A few blocks down at 41 Dunlop Street (near the Perak Street junction) is the **Abdul Gafoor Mosque** (open daily 5am–9.30pm; tel: 6295 4209). Most Singaporean Indians are Hindu, but Muslim Indians congregate here every Friday. You can visit the mosque (except for the prayer hall)

Dramatic figures at the Sri Veeramakaliamman Temple

if you are dressed respectfully. The present brick structure, completed in 1907, features a blend of South Indian and Moorish architectural elements such as arches, onion-shaped domes and ornate ornamentation.

If you are feeling peckish, stop at the vegetarian restaurant **Komala Vilas** (76–8 Serangoon Road; tel: 6293 6980) for a meal of *thosai* (rice-flour pancakes). Returning to Serangoon Road, take a brief detour down Cuff Road to **Ashaweni Mills** (No. 2 Cuff Road; open Mon–Sat 8am–1pm and 2–5pm; tel: 6299 3726). It is a noisy and one of the last remaining traditional spice grinders in Singapore, where the freshest mixes of spices, flours and betel nuts are custom ground.

Sri Veeramakaliamman Temple

A little further up Serangoon Road, next to Belilios Road, is the **Sri Veeramakaliamman Temple** (141 Serangoon Road; open daily 8am–noon and 4–9pm; tel: 6295 4538),

Day of rest

On Sundays, throngs of workers from the Indian subcontinent hang out in Little India on their rest day. Traffic can slow to a crawl, and the streets and shops are packed to the gills.

constructed by Bengalis in 1855. This is one of Singapore's finest Hindu shrines. Dedicated to Kali, the Hindu Goddess of Power, it is packed with devotees on the Hindu holy days of Tuesdays and Fridays. They often break a coconut before entering to denote the breaking of their ego. Cracked shells are tossed into the aluminium receptacles under the *gopuram* tower. The interior is interesting for several Hindu symbols it employs: fresh coconut and mango leaves above the entrance are for purity and welcome; the lotus represents human striving for spiritual perfection; and banana offerings indicate abundance.

On a lighter note is the charming **Museum of Shanghai Toys** (open Tues–Sun 11am–7pm; admission fee: tel: 6294 7747; <www.most.com.sg>) at 83 Rowell Road. The engaging repository of colourful antique tin toys, comic books, dolls and more is the result of one man's loving collection over many years.

The multi-level **Mustafa Centre** (145 Syed Alwi Road; tel: 6295 5855; <www.mustafa.com.sg>), off Serangoon Road near the Farrer Park MRT Station, is open 24 hours, offering a mind-boggling array of goods from groceries to electronic gadgets, all at very good discount prices. Another branch is located nearby in Serangoon Plaza (open daily 10.30am–11.30pm).

Sri Srinivasa Perumal Temple

Near the Farrer Park MRT Station, at 397 Serangoon Road, is another national monument, the **Sri Srinivasa Perumal Temple** (open daily 6.30am–noon and 5–9pm; tel: 6298 5771). Dating from 1855, it has a vast prayer hall that honours Krishna (also known as Perumal), one of the incarnations of Vishnu, the supreme Hindu god. The temple is topped by a five-tier *gopuram* tower, donated by P. Govindasamy Pillai, an early Indian migrant made good.

Buddhist Temples

On nearby Race Course Road, which runs parallel to the west of Serangoon Road, is the **Sakya Muni Buddha Gaya Temple** (No. 366; open daily 8am–4.45pm; tel: 6294 0714), better known as the Temple of 1,000 Lights. This Buddhist shrine, maintained by Thai monks, is one of the most popular religious

The giant Buddha at Sayka Muni Buddha Gaya Temple

shrines in Singapore. Its centrepiece is the seated Buddha statue, 15m (49ft) tall and weighing 305kg (300 tons). It is surrounded by bulbs that light up every time a donation is made. Several Hindu statues and two bright yellow tigers are posted as guards outside.

The temple across the road, at 371 Race Course Road, is **Leong San Buddhist Temple** (Dragon Mountain Temple) (open daily 6am–5.30pm; tel: 6298 9371), a less fanciful place of worship that dates back to the late 1800s, dedicated to Guan Yin, the Goddess of Mercy. It also has an image of Confucius at its altar and is thus popular with parents who bring their children to pray for success in examinations.

KAMPONG GLAM

Named after the *gelam* trees that once grew here, the **Kampong Glam** district (north of the Civic District and the Singapore River) was the historic seat of the Malay sultans. It was settled in the early days by Muslims from the Malay Peninsula and the Bugis from Indonesia. Even today this neighbourhood has maintained a Malay character.

Arab Street

Arab Street is the traditional home of Singapore's textile dealers and there are still many small silk and batik stores as well as sarong shops and tailors here. Leather goods, caneware, fishing gear and shiny metalwork are also for sale in the shophouses and make for an interesting browse. Go early as most shops close after 5pm.

Shoppers in Arab Street

Sultan Mosque

Kampong Glam's leading attraction is the **Sultan Mosque** (3 Muscat Road; open Sat–Thur 9am–noon and 2–4pm, Fri 2.30–4pm; tel: 6293 4405), located between Arab Street and North Bridge Road at the end of Bussorah Street. It is impressive with a massive onion-shaped golden dome and corner minarets. A

The grand Sultan Mosque

national monument that dates back to 1924, this is Singapore's largest mosque; visitors are welcome to view (but not enter) its grand prayer hall.

Malay Heritage Centre

The **Malay Heritage Centre** (open Mon 1–6pm, Tues–Sun 10am–6pm; admission fee; tel: 6391 0450; <www.malay heritage.org.sg>) is housed in the large compound (open daily 8am–9pm; free) of **Istana Kampong Gelam**, the former residence of the son of the first sultan of Singapore, dating back to the 1840s. The museum in the centre has interesting displays tracing the history and heritage of Malays.

To the left of the compound's main gate is the Yellow Mansion or **Gedung Kuning**, the former home of Tengku Mahmoud, grandson of Sultan Hussein. Today it houses a Malay restaurant **Tepak Sireh** (tel: 6396 4373).

Kampong Glam Shopping

At 44 Kandahar Street is **Bumbu** (open Tues–Sun 11am–3pm and 6–10pm; tel: 6392 8628), a Thai-Indonesian restaurant filled with an eclectic collection of rare antiques sourced from

➤

All puffed out

After a day of shopping and sightseeing, unwind at one of the restaurants in Kampong Glam with a puff on a *shisha*, the traditional Middle Eastern water pipe. Try Altazzag Egyptian restaurant (24 Haji Lane; tel: 6295 5024).

various Singaporean homes. Head back to **Bussorah Mall** for a spot of souvenir shopping. **Little Shophouse** (43 Bussorah Street; tel: 6295 2328) sells pretty hand-stitched beaded Peranakan slippers while **Grandfather's Collections** (42 Bussorah Street; tel: 6299 4530) has local vintage treasures. **Jamal Kazura Aromatics Store** (21 Bussorah Street; tel: 6293 2350) has a fine display of decanters as well as alcohol-free perfumes for sale.

Continue shopping in **Haji Lane**, where the old mixes with the new and funky. Most of the trendy hole-in-the-wall boutiques and cafés here open till late. Hip tenants include **Pitch Black** (63 Haji Lane; tel: 6392 3457), a café with a film theatre and art gallery upstairs, and fashion and home accessories stores **Salad** (25/27 Haji Lane; tel: 6299 5805) and **Pluck** (31/33 Haji Lane; tel: 6396 4048).

More Historic Mosques

Right at the corner of Jalan Sultan and Victoria Street is the **Malabar Jamaath Mosque** (471 Victoria Street; open daily 10am–noon, 2–4pm; tel: 6294 3862), famous for its blue tile work. Northeast of the Sultan Mosque, at 4001 Beach Road, is the **Hajjah Fatimah Mosque** (open daily to visitors 9am–9pm; tel: 6297 2774), built in 1846 by the Malay wife of a Bugis merchant as a private residence. Its remarkable architecture mixes European and Chinese influences and it has a Malay-style minaret that resembles the spire of a cathedral. The minaret is off the plumb, leading some to dub it the 'leaning tower of Singapore'.

Bugis

Bugis Street, south of the Arab Street area, was Singapore's most notorious after-dark hangout until it was razed in 1985 to make way for the Bugis MRT station. Now, in place of a street internationally renowned for prostitution and drag queens, there is **Parco Bugis Junction**, a shopping mall with a glassed-over air-conditioned shopping street and the adjoining luxury Hotel InterContinental. Next to the hotel is the stark-white **National Library** (100 Victoria Street; open daily 10am–9pm; free; tel: 6332 3255; <www.nl.sg>). It houses a reference library, restful outdoor gardens, a café, an art exhibition space and the Drama Centre performing arts theatre.

Across Victoria Street is the lively **Bugis Street Market** in the Bugis Village complex. Crammed with over 600 stalls, the market offers value finds such as look-alike Oakleys, cheap, fashionable streetwear and hawker food.

Pluck, a fashion and home accessories store in Haji Lane

Kwan Im Thong Hood
Cho Temple

Waterloo Street

Follow Rochor Road by the side of the Bugis Village complex and turn into the pedestrianised section of **Waterloo Street**. On any given day, this area teems with people who come to pray at the Chinese **Kwan Im Thong Hood Cho Temple** (open daily 6am–6.15pm; tel: 6337 9227) and the Hindu **Sri Krishnan Temple** (open daily 5am–9pm; tel: 6337 7957).

The Buddhist Goddess of Mercy, Guan Yin, presides in the former. Built in 1895 and refurbished in 1982, the temple is a highlight not for its architecture but rather for the glimpses of colourful local life it offers. Pensive supplicants inside the temple kneel before the goddess in prayer. Some shake containers with numbered bamboo fortune sticks until one falls out, then consult with the fortune tellers who stake out outside along with the traditional medicine and flower sellers. From lottery numbers to prospects for offspring, the goddess tries to unravel everything about the future.

Sculpture Square (open Mon–Fri 11am–6pm, Sat–Sun noon–6pm; free; tel: 6333 1055) is housed in a 19th-century church building at the corner of Waterloo Street and Middle Road. It presents interesting three-dimensional art exhibitions.

ORCHARD ROAD

The **Orchard Road** area, roughly from the beginning of
Plaza Singapura near the Dhoby Ghaut MRT Station all the
way to the end of Tanglin Road near the Botanic Gardens,
is Singapore's best known shopping and dining district *(see
pages 84–5, 139–40)*, though it has some sights worth seeing too. The name of this glitzy road goes back to the 1840s
when Captain William Scott established his nutmeg and pepper plantation on the slopes. Tigers roamed the hills along
Orchard Road until 1846; fifty years later, the land was
tamed and some of Singapore's richest families had built their
estates and terrace homes here.

The most notable cluster of these historic residences is on
Emerald Hill, the site of one of Singapore's first and most
impressive preservation projects. A stroll up Emerald Hill
Road from Peranakan Place is a walk into Singapore's colonial past. The terrace houses were built between 1902 and
1930 on the site of a nutmeg farm using a plethora of Malay,
Chinese and European styles. The original owners were
wealthy Peranakan, a mixed race that evolved through intermarriage between immi-
grant Chinese men and local
Malay women from the 17th
to 19th centuries. Pastel
hues, fancy plaster work, ornate grills, shuttered windows, bat-shaped openings,
tiled overhangs and carved
wood characterise many of
these graceful exteriors.
Among the houses are a few
galleries, restaurants and
pubs, which allow a glimpse

Orchard Road, tops for shops

of the colonial-period interiors, but most of the restored terrace houses and shophouses are private residences. The carved swing doors *(pintu pagar)* are designed for ventilation and privacy.

Orchard Road is also the address of the **Istana**, the Singapore president's official residence. In the late 1860s Indian convicts did the heavy work on this government estate, which is closed to visitors except on public holidays such as Chinese New Year's Day, Hari Raya Puasa, Labour Day, Deepavali and National Day (open 8.30am–6pm; <www.istana.gov.sg>). If you are there on the first Sunday of the month, you can catch the changing of the guard at the Istana gates (starting at 6pm).

Chinese Baroque houses on Emerald Hill

Further away but more accessible is the **Goodwood Park Hotel** (22 Scotts Road; tel: 6737 7411; <www.goodwoodparkhotel.com.sg>), a national landmark built in 1900 as the Teutonia Club for German colonialists. The Goodwood vies with the Raffles as Singapore's most luxurious historic hotel. Resembling a Rhineland castle with an eight-sided Bavarian tower, it was occupied by the Japanese during the war and served as the War Crimes Court later. Celebrities who had spent the night here include Anna Pavlova and John Wayne.

GEYLANG SERAI AND KATONG

When the British transformed Singapore into a trading colony, many Malays took up residence in **Geylang Serai**, east of the city centre. The district still has a strong Malay character, complete with old bungalows, terrace houses and Peranakan shophouses, especially along Joo Chiat and Koon Seng roads near the Paya Lebar MRT Station. Singapore's largest red-light district and a cluster of 'love hotels' are located in the *lorong* (alleys) here. Here as well is the colourful **Geylang Serai Market**, located in a new double-storey building on Jalan Turi that was designed to simulate the rustic quality of the old Malay kampong houses.

Malay Village

Dominating this area at 39 Geylang Serai is a white elephant called the **Malay Village**. This sizeable cultural park re-creation of a traditional Malay village of wooden stilt-house architecture, a museum and shops never quite took off and it closed in June 2008. The village currently awaits redevelopment. In the meantime, for a better insight into Malay customs and traditions, head to the museum at the Malay Heritage Centre in Kampong Glam *(see page 55)*.

Katong

North of Geylang Serai, further along Joo Chiat Road, is the **Katong** suburb area. It is historically the heart of the Peranakan community and many of the shophouses here, combining Chinese, Peranakan and European architectural styles, have been conserved. Katong is also a foodie's haven, where you can find some of the best Peranakan restaurants in Singapore. The main spine to explore is East Coast Road. You can spend a day just sampling the many delicious offerings, from the famous spicy Katong laksa noodle dish (try one of the stalls at the corner of Ceylon and East Coast Road) to *kaya* (traditional coconut custard jam) toast at the nostalgic **Chin Mee Chin Confectionery** (204 East Coast Road; open Tues–Sun 8.30am–5pm) and homemade rice dumplings at **Kim Choo Kueh Chang** (109/111 East Coast Road; tel: 6440 5590). To see precious collections of Peranakan family heirlooms, intricately beaded slippers and jewellery, head to **Katong Antique House** (208 East Coast Road; open Tues–Sun 10.30am–6pm; tel: 6345 8544) and **Rumah Bebe** (113 East Coast Road; open Tues–Sun 9.30am–6.30pm; tel: 6247 8781; <www.rumahbebe.com>).

ZOOS, PARKS AND ORCHID GARDENS

Some of Singapore's top attractions are found outside the crowded urbanised centres and downtown Singapore. These include the island's world-renowned zoos, a park devoted to birds, nature reserves and the orchid farms which form a much appreciated counterweight to the city-state's urban landscape.

Singapore Botanic Gardens

The **Singapore Botanic Gardens** (1 Cluny Road; open daily 5am–midnight; free; tel: 6471 7361; <www.sbg.org.sg>), just west of Orchard Road, is the nearest major green preserve to the downtown district. The 67-hectare (166-acre) site of gardens and jungle forests was opened in 1859.

A path begins at Swan Lake, surrounded by palms and rubber trees, then leads past an 1860 bandstand and a topiary garden. The 1.5-hectare (3.7-acre) **Evolution Garden** traces life on earth from 4,600 million years ago till the present day with live exhibits and plant replicas.

A must-visit is the **National Orchid Garden** (open daily 8.30am–7pm; admission fee), located within the Botanic

Gardens, which claims to have the world's largest display of Singapore's signature blooms. It has over 3,000 varieties of orchids, including Singapore's national flower, the purple Vanda Miss Joaquim, which was first discovered in 1893 by an Armenian immigrant, Agnes Joachim. There are also numerous 'VIP' orchids, named after the many dignitaries who have visited Singapore. Located within this garden is the **Cool House**, which encloses a montane tropical forest. The **Taman Serasi Food Garden** near the Cluny Road exit offers cheap local food.

Chinese and Japanese Gardens

Gardens of a different order are maintained at the **Chinese Garden** and **Japanese Garden** (1 Chinese Garden Road; open daily Chinese Garden 6am–10.30pm, Bonsai Garden 9am–5pm, Japanese Garden 6am–7pm; free tel: 6261 3632).

The vandaceous orchid hybrid *Aranda* Noorah Alsagoff

Chinese Garden pavilions

The Chinese Garden reflects several classical styles and has twin pagodas, arched bridges, an extensive *bonsai* display, elaborate rock works, a teahouse and even a marble boat like the one in Beijing's Summer Palace gardens. The garden is decorated with colourful lanterns in September/October for the annual Mid Autumn Festival. From the Chinese Garden visitors can cross a bridge into the Japanese Garden with its carefully raked Zen rock gardens, stone lanterns, pavilions and pools.

Haw Par Villa

Far livelier than the Chinese and Japanese Gardens is the most Chinese of Singapore's theme parks, **Haw Par Villa**, also known as Tiger Balm Gardens (262 Pasir Panjang Road; open daily 9am–7pm; free; tel: 6872 2780). There is hardly a native resident in Singapore who hasn't been taken here as a child. This park was opened in 1937 by local millionaire Aw Boon Haw, who built a mansion for his younger brother,

Aw Boon Par, on the summit. The Aws made a vast fortune that was based, in large part, on sales of the famous Tiger Balm ointment. The Japanese destroyed the mansion during their occupation (1942–5) and it was never replaced, but the park itself was rebuilt. The government acquired it in 1985 and leased it to a private firm that tried to update the old theme park with high-tech displays and rides. This renovation was a failure, and Haw Par Villa has now returned to its roots.

The amusement park lining the slopes below the villa is lined with garish and often grotesque statuary, telling stories from classical Chinese mythology, literature and folklore. For generations parents have brought their children here to expose them to traditional values – mostly Confucian – behind these stories. The statues originally numbered over a thousand and there were scores of colourful and striking tableaux showing fantastic heroes and villains representing aspects of good and evil, engaged in the primal struggles of life and death.

The best sights in the park are the huge tableaux of classic Chinese stories that stand at the summit and the cave called the **Ten Courts of Hell** (admission fee), where appropriate punishments for earthly sins are gruesomely and surrealistically inflicted on life-size figures by their tormentors. **Hua Song Museum** (open daily 9am–6pm; admission fee; tel: 6339 6833; <www.huasong. org>), located within the park, has eight galleries tracing the history of the Chinese diaspora.

Dragon slayer at Haw Par Villa

Jurong BirdPark

The largest bird park in Southeast Asia, **Jurong BirdPark** (2 Jurong Hill; open daily 9am–6pm; admission fee; tel: 6265 0022; <www.birdpark.com.sg>) is located on 20 hectares (50 acres) of parkland far west of downtown. More than 9,000 birds, representing 600 species, reside here. Its Southeast Asian hornbill collection is the largest in the world. Also the largest in the world is a 30-m (98-ft)-high artificial waterfall at the end of a walk-in aviary, where 1,500 birds fly freely.

It is best to arrive early before the heat gets too much. The park can be explored on foot, but there is a panorail (admission fee) that links the myriad displays. Among the more notable displays are the **Southeast Asian Birds Aviary**, where a tropical thunderstorm is simulated at noon; the **World of Darkness** nocturnal house, where snowy owls, night herons and kiwis can be observed in darkness; and a **Parrot Paradise** with the park's most colourful and friendly residents. Other attractions include a lake with over 1,000 pink flamingos and the entertaining **Birds 'n Buddies Show** (daily 11am and 3pm)

The Feather in Singapore's Cap

Although a concrete island of high-rises, Singapore has more than 350 species of birds to delight even the most casual bird-watcher. Early morning, around 7am, is prime spotting time. A good place to start a bird-watching expedition is at the Visitor Centre in the Bukit Timah Nature Reserve, where illustrated field guides are for sale. The Sungei Buloh Nature Park on the northwestern coast has observation blinds by mangroves where there's a breeding colony of herons in residence from August to March. Pulau Ubin, with its mangroves and rainforests, is home to parakeets, owls, kingfishers and hornbills. And from September to March, the white cattle egret takes its winter holiday in Singapore, arriving from as far north as Japan and as far west as France.

at the Pools Amphitheatre. At the **Fuji Hawk Walk**, you can catch eagles, falcons and hawks swooping and soaring during the **Birds of Prey** show (10am and 4pm). Another display, **The Riverine**, offers a river's edge view of over 20 duck species fishing and nesting in a pristine niche. Their underwater activities, including diving for fish, can be observed through a wide glass portal on a path that runs below the river's surface. A recreated **African Wetlands** and the **Pelican Cove**, where visitors can view underwater feeding of pelicans, are other recent additions.

A human perch at the Jurong BirdPark

Bukit Timah Nature Reserve

The **Bukit Timah Nature Reserve** (177 Hindhede Drive; open daily 8.30am–6.30pm; free; tel: 6468 5736), located in the northern part of the island, is easily reached by taking a taxi.

This spacious park, occupying 163 hectares (403 acres), harbours Singapore's largest surviving virgin lowland rainforest, native vegetation that once covered most of the island. Bukit Timah is a marvellous place to hike, with a series of well-marked trails winding through the hillsides. Bukit Timah is the name of the park's summit, the highest point in Singapore at a modest 164m (538ft).

Bukit Timah boasts more tree species than the whole of North America. The towering tropical trees provide a canopy for palms, rattans and over 80 species of ferns. Flying lemurs, long-tailed macaques, pangolins (spiny anteaters), mouse deer, giant forest ants, banded woodpeckers and tit babblers are sometimes heard but not often seen.

The Visitor Centre (open daily 8.30am–6pm) at the park entrance has hiking maps and an exhibition on the park's ecosystem. An uphill hike from the centre to the Summit Hut, with its picnic shelter and lookout on stilts, takes under 30 minutes. The four main walking trails (and side trails) lead to valleys and large quarries. There is also a 6-km (4-mile) biking trail.

MacRitchie Reservoir Park

The **MacRitchie Reservoir Park** (open 24 hours daily; free), located in the Central Catchment Nature Reserve along

Common treeshew at the Bukit Timah Nature Reserve

Lornie Road, is another scenic spot for nature lovers. Board-walks and walking trails, ranging from 3 to 11km (2 to 7 miles), skirt the edge of the reservoir and through the flour-ishing forest. The **TreeTop Walk** (open Tues–Fri 9am–5pm, Sat–Sun 8.30am–5pm; free; tel: 6468 5736) offers good views of the forest canopy from dizzying heights of up to 25m (82ft). This 250-m (820-ft)-long suspension bridge con-nects the two highest points in the reservoir park. To get there, you must first hike through a 4½-km (3-mile) nature trail. The TreeTop Walk is especially popular at weekends, and with only 30 people allowed on the bridge at any one time, the wait to get on can be long. Go on a weekday to avoid the crowds.

Mandai Orchid Gardens

Singapore's most often-visited flower farm is the **Mandai Orchid Gardens** (open Mon 8am–6pm, Tues–Sun 8am–7pm; admission fee; tel: 6269 1036; <www.mandai.com.sg>) on 200 Mandai Lake Road, well north of the downtown area, near the zoo. Operated by a private grower, the Mandai Or-chid Gardens exports cut flowers and plants to over 30 coun-tries worldwide. The water garden includes tropical plants from many countries that do well in Singapore's climate, in-cluding heliconia and traveller's palm. Gardeners are usually hard at work tending the orchids, which require intensive cul-tivation. Organic herbs and vegetables grown in the garden are also served in the restaurant here.

Singapore Zoo

The **Singapore Zoo** on 80 Mandai Lake Road (open daily 8.30am–6pm; tel: 6269 3411; admission fee; <www.zoo.com.sg>), north of downtown, houses over 3,000 animals and reptiles on its 28 hectares (69 acres). Its 'open zoo' concept sets it apart from other zoos. Cleverly concealed features, including moats, cascading streams and vegetation, help serve as barriers, although a few glass-fronted enclosures are employed for species that can leap over walls. Some 'lucky' animals, including langurs, lemurs and tamarins, are allowed to roam freely around the zoo.

Not to be missed are the animal shows, staged six times daily in selected areas. Most shows are held in the Shaw Foundation Amphitheatre, where sea lions, reptiles and primates take their turns on stage throughout the day. The elephant shows take place at the Elephants of Asia enclosure. An animal show specially designed to entertain children gets under way at the new Rainforest Kidzworld daily. Note, too, that many animals, from lions and jaguars to monkeys and Komodo dragons, are fed on a regular schedule (times posted at the zoo entrance) and this can often lead to exciting impromptu shows. Even the tigers are likely to take a plunge in their pool when the feeding crew arrives.

The zoo also provides a splendid opportunity to have a meal in close proximity to the animals. If you fancy having a **Jungle Breakfast** (9–10am daily; fee) among orang-utans (the zoo's colony is the largest in the world) and other wildlife, book a place at the Jungle Flavours restaurant in advance. Or get to feed some rare Hamadryas baboons when you hop on a buggy for the hour-long **Wild Discoverer Tour** (11am, 2pm and 4pm daily; fee) into the heart of the forest.

To avoid the crowds, make your zoo visit in the morning on a weekday. If you are combining a visit with the Night Safari next door (highly recommended), it is best to take your zoo tour in the afternoon, three to four hours before the 6pm closing time and then walk over to the Night Safari for dinner before the guided tram tours commence at 7.30pm. Both the zoo and the Night Safari are crowded all day every day, as these are two of Singapore's top attractions.

Hippo residents of the Singapore Zoo

Night Safari

The world's first night zoo, Singapore's **Night Safari** (80 Mandai Lake Road; open daily 7.30pm–midnight; retail shops open from 6pm; tel: 6269 3411; <www.nightsafari. com.sg>; admission fee) is the island nation's top attraction. Covering 40 hectares (99 acres), it is a completely different experience. Beginning at dusk (7.30pm), a series of trams with witty English-speaking narrators aboard, encircles the eight geographical zones on a 3.2-km (2-mile) paved road. Passengers can disembark to take a closer look at the animals in their open enclosures by following one of three walking trails (Fishing Cat, Leopard and Forest Giants).

Set in a dense tropical forest, next to an inlet of the Seletar Reservoir, the Night Safari is a subtly lit preserve inhabited by more than 900 animals from about 130 species found in Asia, Africa and South America. More than 90 percent of the animals in the wild are nocturnal, so this is a chance to see how the animals behave after the heat and sunlight have vanished.

Perhaps the most entertaining creatures are the fishing cats, which are slightly larger than domestic felines. These take the plunge to capture trout in a small stream just inches from the pedestrian bridge that passes through their wooded area. The focused, incandescent lighting used to illuminate the fishing cats and other animals makes everything visible to humans but does not distract the creatures of the night, who are often quite active and seemingly unaware of passers-by. Visitors are separated by natural barriers (moats, vegetation, near-invisible wires), and the lighting system resembles moonlight. Cameras are allowed but flash is prohibited.

The night safari stays open until midnight and many visitors find the later hours less crowded and more interesting.

Wartime Memories

Singapore has a number of museums dedicated to the events of World War II. **Memories At Old Ford Factory** (351 Upper Bukit Timah Road; open Mon–Fri 9am–5.30pm, Sat 9am–1.30pm; admission fee; tel: 6462 6724; <www.s1942.org.sg>) in the historic Ford factory is the site where the British surrendered to the Japanese on 15 February 1942. Nearby is **Reflections at Bukit Chandu** (31-K Pepys Road; open Tues–Sun 9am–5pm; tel: 6375 2510; admission fee), a memorial to the Malay soldiers who fought against the Japanese. The **Labrador Secret Tunnel** (open daily 10am–7pm, guided tours every hour; admission fee; tel: 6339 6833), in Labrador Park at Labrador Villa Road off Pasir Panjang Road, takes you through two World War II tunnels. On the eastern side of Singapore is the **Changi Museum** (1000 Upper Changi Road North; open daily 9.30am–5pm, last admission 4.30pm; free; tel: 6214 2451; <www.changimuseum.com>), a small museum dedicated to prisoners of war.

ISLAND EXCURSIONS

Singapore is an island of islands. Some of its 63 nearby islets are now used for petroleum refining and storage, but a few make for excellent day trips.

The Sentosa Express and Merlion statue

Sentosa

Sentosa (admission fee; tel: 1800-736 8672; <www.sentosa.com.sg>), just south of the main island, is connected by the 710-m (½-mile) Causeway Bridge (open to cars and taxis from 7am until midnight daily). A more exciting way of getting there is to take a **cable car** ride that drifts 60m (197ft) above the harbour into the heart of the island. Cable cars depart continuously from **HarbourFront Tower 2**, from 8.30am daily; the last cable cars return from Sentosa at 11pm. Cable cars depart from The Jewel Box on Mount Faber as well; these also offer 'sky dining' from 6.30 to 8.30pm daily (tel: 6377 9688; <www.mountfaber.com.sg>). The fastest mode of transport to the island is the light rail **Sentosa Express**. Board from the Sentosa Express station located in VivoCity shopping mall on the main island (first train 7am, last train midnight). The Sentosa Express stops at two stations on Sentosa, which are within walking distance of many attractions. Otherwise, you can connect to shuttle buses and trams (free) to get to the attractions.

Sentosa served as the headquarters of the British military in the 18th century. Formerly known as Pulau Blakang

The Sentosa Luge & Skyride

Mati ('island at the back of which lies death'), the island was renamed Sentosa ('isle of peace and tranquillity') in 1972 and developed as a resort.

Visitors may find the theme island too much like a hygienic Disneyland to be interesting, but to be fair, Sentosa's recreational opportunities are among Singapore's best. There are some historical and cultural attractions that are worth touring in their own right. To revitalise some of the faded attractions, the authorities are spending a whopping S$8 billion on a 10-year development plan to be completed by 2012. Sentosa Cove, a premier oceanfront residential site, and a family-friendly integrated resort with a Universal Studios theme park and a casino are under development.

Many of the attractions levy additional admission fees. Package tickets can be purchased at the cable car ticketing counters at HarbourFront Tower 2 and on Mount Faber as well as at the Beach and VivoCity Sentosa Express stations.

Many of the main attractions are grouped in a cluster named the **Imbiah Lookout**, near the Imbiah Station and the cable car station. Here the 131-m (430-ft)-high **Carlsberg Sky Tower** (open 9am–9pm daily; admission fee) gives a bird's eye view of the Singapore skyline and the nearby southern islands. Alternatively, at the 37-m (120-ft)-high **Sentosa Merlion** statue (open 10am–8pm daily; admission fee), elevators whisk visitors to its crown and mouth. From the crown, there is a fine view of the island and the busy harbour. At night, the Merlion becomes the focus of a light show, complete with smoke and laser lights worthy of a psychedelic half-fish, half-lion.

Visitors with children may want to head to kid-friendly attractions such as the **Butterfly Park & Insect Kingdom** (open daily 9am–6.30pm; admission fee) with over 1,500 butterflies and an exhibit of unusual insects, the interactive **Sentosa 4D Magix** movie theatre (first show 10am, last show 8.30pm; admission fee), the **Sentosa CineBlast** with cinema simulation rides (daily 10am–9pm; admission fee) and the **Sentosa Luge & Skyride** (daily 10am–9.30pm; admission fee). Sentosa's best attraction in Imbiah Lookout is **Images of Singapore** (open daily 9am–7pm; admission fee), a fine wax museum housed in the colonial-style, former military hospital. This tells of Singapore's history and displays its various cultures using life-sized dioramas, artefacts, films and replicas of old street scenes.

Sentosa has some of Singapore's best beaches

Songs of the Sea multimedia extravaganza at Siloso Beach

Sentosa's other historical display is **Fort Siloso Tours** (open daily 10am–6pm; admission fee). The original fort was built by the British in the 1880s for Singapore's defence. The interactive displays along the underground passages, the cannons and guns, and the video games tell the fort's history from its construction through to its fall in World War II. Also here are the **Surrender Chambers**, which bring to life Singapore's formal surrender to the Japanese in 1942 with a mix of gripping audio-visual footage, artefacts and realistic wax figurines.

The **Underwater World** (open daily 9am–9pm; admission fee includes that for the Dolphin Lagoon) is a small but excellent oceanarium with a submerged acrylic tunnel in its main tank. Visitors go through the tunnel on a travellator, with 2,500 sea creatures – including turtles, stingrays, sharks, sea cows and monstrous eels overhead and on all sides. The Underwater World also oversees the **Dolphin**

Lagoon (open daily 10.30am–6pm) at Palawan Beach, where you can enjoy a show and come face to face with Indo-Pacific Humpback Dolphins, also known as pink dolphins for their unique coloration.

Sentosa is also popular for its beaches. The sands are soft and clean at **Palawan Beach** and **Siloso Beach**, which have good beach bars as well as sailboards, canoes and pedal boats for hire. At Siloso Beach a multimedia extravaganza conceptualised by acclaimed designer Yves Pepin, **Songs of the Sea** (admission fee), dazzles audiences every evening at 7.40pm and 8.40pm. Actors perform with shooting jets of water, fire and laser lights to a rousing musical score.

Southern Islands

Nearby **Kusu Island** and **St John's Island** offer escapes for Singapore residents. St John's, the larger of the two, has little else besides picnicking and swimming, although its concrete promenades on the shoreline are fine for strolls and for watching the heavy ship traffic. For overnight stays, a holiday bungalow is available. (For bookings, call tel: 1800-736 8672).

Kusu, also called Turtle Island, has more to see. Legend has it that two shipwrecked sailors – one Chinese, one Malay – were saved when a giant turtle transformed itself into an island. Each man gave thanks according to his own belief, and so today the Taoist **Tua Pek Kong Temple**, with its turtle pool, and the Muslim keramat (shrine) on the hill are popular places of pilgrimage. In the ninth month of the lunar calendar, usually straddling October and November, Taoists and Buddhists as well as Malays flock to the island. The Chinese come to pray for prosperity, good luck and fertility, while Malay pilgrims climb the 152 steps to the shrine to offer their prayers to Allah.

The ferry (tel: 6534 9339; <www.islandcruise.com.sg>) to both islands departs Mon–Fri at 10am and 2pm, Sat at 9am, noon and 3pm, Sun and holidays at 9am, 11am, 1pm, 3pm and 5pm, from the Marina South Pier. (To get to the pier, take bus number 402 from the Marina Bay MRT Station.) The last ferry departs St John's at 2.45pm (Sat 3.45pm, Sun 5.50pm) and Kusu at 4pm (Sat 4.30pm, Sun 6.15pm).

Pulau Ubin

If time allows a visit to only one of Singapore's little islands, the best choice is **Pulau Ubin** (Granite Island), where some of the last vestiges of old Singapore hang on by their fingertips. Part of the fun is getting there, on a bumboat from the Changi Point Ferry Terminal (accessible by taxi or take the MRT to the Tanah Merah station, then bus number 2). The bumboat takes about 10 minutes to make the crossing. The first boat leaves Singapore at 6.30am and the last leaves Pulau Ubin at 10pm. (There is no fixed schedule; the boat departs as soon as it has 12 passengers. Make special arrangements with the boatman if you are leaving late.)

The village at the wharf on Pulau Ubin consists of a cluster of *kelong* (Malay fishing huts) and several businesses renting bicycles, which are ideal for getting around this little island. An information kiosk (open daily 8.30am–5pm; tel: 6542 4108) at the village entrance provides useful maps

Chek Jawa

Another excellent spot to enjoy Pulau Ubin's nature offerings is Chek Jawa on the southeastern tip. The intertidal mudflats here are so fertile that they have engendered a rich ecosystem found nowhere else in Singapore. A boardwalk and seven-storey viewing tower were added in 2007 to help visitors better appreciate the reserve. The two-hour guided tour must be booked in advance (tel: 6542 4108).

and offers the guided 1½-hour **Sensory Trail** (maximum 15 persons; admission fee; tel: 6542 4108; <www.nparks.gov.sg>). You can also go on this signposted trail on your own. It will guide you to feel the texture of lichen and banana bark as you walk among overhanging tendrils of aerial roots. You will be able to touch, see and smell fruit trees, spices and herbs used in cooking and medicine, and native plants of the mangrove forest. The trail does not cover a large area but it rewards exploration.

Cycling in rural Pulau Ubin

Otherwise, hire a bicycle for the day. Ride past mangrove swamps, coconut palm groves, fruit trees, granite quarries, and rustic duck and prawn farms. Brahminy kites and white-bellied fish eagles are fairly common and easy to spot as they soar on the rising air currents along the foreshore. Long-tailed macaques and wild boars also live here but they are harder to find. Some residents still farm and fish, others serve the tourist trade and a few run seafood restaurants near the jetty.

For those who wish to spend the night, accommodation is available at **MCC Ubin Resort** (tel: 6388 8388; <www.marinacountryclub.com.sg>). Alternatively, overnight camping is allowed on **Noordin Beach** and **Mamam Beach** and the new **Jelutong** campsite; no visitor's permit is required.

WHAT TO DO

Shopping and eating are the lifeblood of Singapore. Visitors will find an endless array of places to do both, economically or in high style. There is also an increasing number of venues for entertainment and sports as well as an extensive calendar of annual festivals. And no other city offers a better opportunity to introduce children to the cultures of Asia.

SHOPPING

If Singapore has a national pastime, it is shopping. The downtown is stuffed with air-conditioned malls, department stores and boutiques, and the ethnic neighbourhoods offer additional street markets and unique shops. Most shopping centres and shops are open from 10am to 9pm daily (sometimes later at weekends). Credit cards are widely accepted. Bargaining is not practised at most of the larger stores but vendors with stalls in markets often do. Many retailers can provide overseas shipping. Insist on written confirmation of your purchases and buy shipping insurance unless your credit card covers it.

Prices for many goods in Singapore are equal to or higher than those in Western countries. One of the best times to shop is the **Great Singapore Sale** (<www.greatsingapore sale.com.sg>), which runs from the last week of May through June and July. There are good discounts on a wide range of goods during these eight weeks.

Tax-free Shopping
Singapore offers a great deal of tax-free shopping. Although a Goods and Services Tax (GST) of 7 percent is levied on most

Arab Street shop spilling over with handicrafts

Little India fabric vendor

purchases, this can be refunded if you spend a minimum of S$100 at shops participating in the **Global Refund Scheme** (tel: 6225 6238); <www.globalrefund. com>) or the **Premier Tax Free Scheme** (tel: 6293 3811); <www.premiertax free.com>). Look out for shops with the 'Tax-Free Shopping' or 'Premier Tax Free' sticker. Fill in a voucher for your purchases. Before your departure, validate the voucher at the airport customs, then present it together with your purchased items at the Global Refund counter or Premier Tax Free Scheme counter. You can opt for cash or cheque refund, or ask for the refund to be credited to your credit card or bank account. Global Refund also has a Downtown Cash Refund counters in Funan DigitaLife Mall, Wisma Atria, Centrepoint and Sim Lim Square.

Where to Shop
Civic District
The **Civic District** is dominated by shopping centres and department stores. Among the biggest is **Suntec City Mall** (3 Temasek Boulevard; tel: 6825 2667; <www.sunteccity. com.sg>). It is divided into four zones, with lifestyle products in one and food courts and expensive boutiques in others. French hypermart **Carrefour** (01-199; tel: 6333 6868)

offers reasonably priced groceries, apparel and electronics. The central circular **Fountain of Wealth** is billed as the world's largest fountain; its waters flow downwards instead of shooting upwards, since the traditional Chinese belief is that water represents wealth and the tenants here want the water flowing directly into their shopping centre. Other large malls and shopping arcades in this area include **Millenia Walk** (9 Raffles Boulevard; tel: 6883 1122; <www.millenia walk.com>) and **Marina Square** (6 Raffles Boulevard; tel: 6339 8787; <www.marinasquare.com.sg>).

The **Raffles Hotel Shopping Arcade** (328 North Bridge Road) has art galleries and luxury-brand boutiques, and Raffles Hotel souvenirs are available at its museum shop. The **Raffles City Shopping Centre** (252 North Bridge Road; tel: 6318 0238; <www.rafflescity.com>) nearby is linked to Suntec City Mall by an air-conditioned walkway and shopping mall, appropriately dubbed the **CityLink Mall** (1 Raffles Link; tel: 6339 9913; <www.citylinkmall.com>).

Money-Back Guarantees

Merchants at Changi Airport offer two guarantees. The first is on price. If you find you have paid more at the airport than at one of the downtown department stores and major shops on their list, they will give you a refund that is double the price difference if you can show written proof. The second guarantee is simpler. If you've bought the wrong gift or changed your mind, they will give you a full refund, no questions asked, if you return the item and receipt within 30 days. You can do this even after leaving Singapore; shipping costs will be refunded as well. For details, fax or write to the manager of the airport shop you bought the item from. For details, contact the Civil Aviation Authority of Singapore at fax: 6543 2853; email: <caas_changi_airport_shopping@caas.gov.sg> or look up <www.changiairportshopping.com>.

Near Raffles City on Stamford Road are **Stamford House** (39 Stamford Road) and **Capitol Building** (11 Stamford Road), both with art galleries and fashion boutiques owned by local designers. The **Museum Shop By Banyan Tree** (<www.museumshop.com.sg>) at the National Museum (93 Stamford Road), Singapore Art Museum (71 Bras Basah Road) and the Asian Civilisations Museum (1 Empress Place) specialises in gifts and cultural souvenirs.

Other major malls include **Funan DigitaLife Mall** (109 North Bridge Road; tel: 6336 8327; <www.funan.com.sg>) and **Sim Lim Square** (1 Rochor Canal; tel: 6338 3859; <www.simlimsquare.com.sg>), both packed with computer and electronics stores. **Bugis Junction** (200 Victoria Street; tel: 6557 6557; <www.bugisjunction-mall.com.sg>) is a glass-covered mall that retains its shophouse architecture; across the street from it is the **Bugis Street market**.

Orchard Road

Orchard Road is another major downtown shopping strip, renowned for its upscale international stores. Among the largest shopping malls are **Wisma Atria** (435 Orchard Road; tel: 6235 2103; <www.wismaonline.com>), noted for its fashion boutiques; **Ngee Ann City** (391 Orchard Road; tel: 6506 0461; <www.ngeeanncity.com.sg>), with the Japanese department store Takashimaya; **Paragon** (290 Orchard Road; tel: 6738 5535), with numerous luxury boutiques; and **Centrepoint** (176 Orchard Road; tel: 6737 9000; <www.centrepoint.com.sg>), long a fav-

Late night shopping

Here's another reason to stay up late – some 250 shops and F&B outlets in Orchard Road malls such as Wisma Atria and Centrepoint open until midnight every last Friday of the month, under the Singapore Tourism Board's Friday Late Night Shopping scheme.

ourite of Singaporeans. **Far East Plaza** (14 Scotts Road; tel: 6734 6837) has trendy streetwear at low prices. Two popular home-grown emporiums are **Tangs** (320 Orchard Road; tel: 6737 5500; <www.tangs.com>) with well-loved fashion, beauty and household sections, and **Robinsons**, Singapore's oldest department store located at Centrepoint.

The large red building called the **DFS Galleria** (25 Scotts Road; tel: 6229 8100; <www.dfsgalleria.com>) is a treasure trove of designer fashion and cosmetics with duty-free savings. Slightly further away **Tanglin Shopping Centre** (19 Tanglin Road; tel: 6737 0849) has the city's largest selection of Persian rugs, old maps and Asian antiques.

Bustling Orchard Road

Chinatown

Singapore's ethnic neighbourhoods offer more unusual shopping possibilities. **Chinatown** is headlined by **Yue Hwa Emporium** (70 Eu Tong Sen Street; tel: 6538 4222; <www.yuehwa.com.sg>), a department store where all the clothing, household goods and crafts are from Taiwan and China. **People's Park Centre** (101 Upper Cross Street) is filled with Chinese vendors willing to bargain while **People's Park Complex** (Blk 32 New Market Road) has fabrics and streetwear at good prices.

Henna tattooist in Little India

Little India

Little India is the area to poke around for bangles, gold jewellery, silk saris and Indian spices. **Little India Arcade** on 48 Serangoon Road has over 50 small shops and the nearby **Tekka Centre** (665 Buffalo Road), relocated at Race Course Road till 2010, has a wet market and scores of shops selling saris, batiks, clothing and brassware. **Mustafa Centre** (145 Syed Alwi Road; tel: 6295 5855; <www.mustafa.com.sg>) is a large 24-hour department store popular for its low-priced electronic goods, groceries, garments and knick-knacks.

Suburbs

VivoCity (1 HarbourFront Walk; tel: 6377 6860; <www.vivo city.com.sg>), a shopping and entertainment centre located next to the HarbourFront Centre, was designed by the renowned Japanese architect Toyo Ito and built at a cost of S$280 million. It is the largest retail venue in Singapore at

102,000 sq m (1.1 million sq ft), with top boutiques, cine-plexes, a hypermarket and an excellent bookstore, PageOne.

Suburban malls offer many of the same goods available downtown, but often at much better prices. **Century Square** (2 Tampines Central 5; tel: 6789 6261) is beside the Tampines MRT Station; **Junction 8** (9 Bishan Place; tel: 6354 2955; <www.junction8.com.sg>) is served by the Bishan MRT Station; and **IMM** (Jurong East Street 21) is located across the Jurong East MRT Station.

Specialist Shops
Antiques and Handicrafts

Shoppers for Buddhist art and antiques should check out **Lopburi Arts & Antiques** (01-03/04, Tanglin Place, 91 Tanglin Road; tel: 6738 3834). Shipping and certificates of authenticity are provided. There is a cluster of antique shops at **Tanglin Shopping Centre** (19 Tanglin Road), including **Antiques of the Orient** (02-40; tel: 6734 9351; <www.aoto.com.sg>), **Akemi Gallery** (02-06; tel: 6735 6315), **Hassan's Carpets** (01-12; tel: 6737 5626; <www.hassanscarpets.com>), **Naga Arts & Antiques** (01-49; tel: 6235 7084; <www.nagaarts.com>) and **Renee Hoy Fine Arts** (01-44; tel: 6235 1596). Nearby **Antiquity Hands of the Hills** carries Himalayan and Tibetan pieces (Tudor Court, 141

Complaints Departments

Singapore has several means to rectify retailer malfeasance. You can lodge complaints with the Singapore Tourism Board by calling its hotline 1800-736 2000 (toll-free in Singapore), or contact the Small Claims Tribunal (1st level, Subordinate Courts, 1 Havelock Square; tel. 6435 5946; fax 6435 5994; <www.smallclaims.gov.sg>). At the latter, complaints are heard on short notice and judgements are rendered on the spot.

Tanglin Road; tel: 6735 5332). **Dempsey Road (Tanglin Village)**, near the Botanic Gardens, is also filled with many tiny antique and Asian collectible shops. **Kwok Gallery** (03-01 Far East Shopping Centre, 545 Orchard Road; tel: 6235 2516) has dealt in genuine Chinese pieces since 1918. **Pagoda Street** and **Mosque Street** in Chinatown are also well known for their antique stores.

Further afield, **Singapore Handicrafts** (72 Eunos Avenue 7; tel: 6747 7666; <www.singhandicrafts.com.sg>) stocks a good range of Chinese carvings, paintings and furniture.

Bookstores

Singapore's leading bookstores are **Borders** (01-00 Wheelock Place, 501 Orchard Road; tel: 6235 7146), **Kinokuniya** (03-10/15 Ngee Ann City, 391 Orchard Road; tel: 6737 5021 and 03-09/12 Bugis Junction, 200 Victoria Street; tel: 6339 1790) and **PageOne** (02-41/42 VivoCity, 1 HarbourFront Walk; tel: 6272 0822). The small, independent **Select Books** (03-15 Tanglin Shopping Centre, 19 Tanglin Road; tel: 6732 1515; <www.selectbooks.com.sg>) has a rich collection of Singapore and Southeast Asian books.

Tailors

Coloc Tailor (02-29 Raffles Hotel Arcade, 328 North Bridge Road; tel: 6338 9767; <www.coloc.com.sg>) can complete a suit in 24 hours. **Gentlemen Quarters** (03-13 OUB Centre, 1 Raffles Place; tel: 6532 5526) provides overseas shipping. **Pimab's** (32B Boat Quay; tel: 6538 6466; <www.pimabs.com>), helmed by local fashion designer Leslie Chia, specialises in bespoke services for men at reasonable prices.

ENTERTAINMENT

In addition to the shopping, eating and cultural attractions of Singapore, Singapore has a thriving nightlife scene, although it remains a tamer one than those found in some other Asian and Western capitals.

Performing Arts

Singapore's impresarios bring in performances by international groups and artists. Current attractions are listed in tourist magazines such as *Where Singapore* and in the dailies. Tickets can be purchased at SISTIC (tel: 6348 5555) or tickets.com (tel: 6296 2929) outlets; bookings can also be made at <www.sistic.com.sg> or <www.tdc.sg>. The **Singapore Arts Festival** (<www.singapore-artsfest.com>), organised by the National Arts Council annually in June, is well regarded for its line-up of innovative works.

Chinese opera performers

The **Fort Canning Centre** hosts outdoor performances such as rock concerts and ballets. Singapore has some Chinese opera companies, which often perform on outdoor stages in Chinatown and at annual festivals, particularly during the Festival of the Hungry Ghosts around August. The **Chinese Opera Teahouse** (5

Smith Street; tel: 6323 4862; <www.ctcopera.com.sg>) offers performances of opera excerpts with English subtitles (showtimes Fri and Sat 7–9pm; admission fee inclusive of set dinner).

The iconic **Esplanade – Theatres on the Bay** (1 Esplanade Drive; tel: 6828 8222; <www.esplanade.com>) is Singapore's world-class performing arts centre, a landmark that is hoped will rival the Sydney Opera House. Music, theatre, dance and outdoor performances are hosted in this large complex. The noted **Singapore Symphony Orchestra** performs here regularly; check <www.sso.org.sg> for programme updates.

Nightlife

With hundreds of clubs, bars, and karaoke lounges, late-night entertainment options in Singapore are plenty. The dress code is slightly formal; no sandals, shorts or T-shirts are allowed.

Singapore River

For those seeking a leisurely drink, Singapore has a large number of chic bars and lounges, many with outdoor seating. The **Boat Quay** shophouses are home to a few such establishments. **Harry's Bar** (28 Boat Quay; tel: 6538 3029; <www.harrys. com.sg>) and **Jazz@Southbridge** (82B Boat Quay; tel: 6327 4671; <www.southbridgejazz.com.sg>) offer live jazz. **Molly Malone's Irish Pub** (56 Circular Road; tel: 6536 2029; <www. molly-malone.com>) and the very Victorian **Penny Black** (26–27 Boat Quay; tel: 6538 2300; <www.pennyblack. com.sg>) are excellent places to down pints of Guinness. **Archipelago Craft Beer Hub** (79 Circular Road; tel: 6327 8408; <www.archipelagobrewery.com>) combines beer with local flavours like lemongrass and tamarind. Just across the river is **Bar Opiume** (1 Empress Place Waterfront; tel: 6339 2876), a sophisticated chill-out place stylish to the core.

Upriver is **Clarke Quay** (tel: 6337 3292; <www.clarke

quay.com.sg>) with a slew of hip restaurants, bars and dance clubs like **Attica** (01-03, 3A River Valley; tel: 6333 9973; <www.attica.com.sg>) and **Ministry of Sound** (01-02 Block C, The Cannery; tel: 6235 2292; <www.ministryofsound.com.sg>) from London. At 3,700 sq m (40,000 sq ft), it is the biggest MOS in Asia. Other sexy new kids on the block include **Kandi Bar** (01-06 Block C, The Cannery; tel: 6887 3733; <www.hedkandi.com.sg>) and **Fashion Bar** (01-02A Block C, The Cannery; tel: 6887 3733; <www.fbar.com.sg>).

CHIJMES, a popular nightspot

But what is really unmissable is the top club **Zouk** (17–21 Jiak Kim Street; tel: 6738 2988; <www.zoukclub.com.sg>). Ever the trendsetter, it features a wine bar, three clubs and an annual roster of international celebrity DJs.

Civic District

CHIJMES (30 Victoria Street) is a popular nightlife zone with a number of restaurant and drinking holes, including **Insomnia** (tel: 6338 6883; <www.liverockmusic247.com>), which serves international cuisine in a courtyard under the stars and has good dance and live music all night long.

Other popular Civic District haunts are **Paulaner Bräuhaus** (01-01/02 Time Square@Millenia Walk; tel: 6883 2572; <www.paulaner.com.sg>) and the very stylish **Balaclava**

(01-01B Suntec City; tel: 6339 1600). At the **Long Bar** (Raffles Hotel, 1 Beach Road; tel: 6337 1886), Singapore Slings are must-haves, and the vertigo-inducing **New Asia Bar** at Swissôtel The Stamford (71st & 72nd Floors, 2 Stamford Road; tel: 6837 3322) offers fabulous views of the city.

Orchard Road

On **Emerald Hill** beside the Centrepoint Shopping Centre are several hot spots. The Spanish-inspired wine bar **Que Pasa** (7 Emerald Hill Road; tel: 6235 6626) serves sangria and delicious tapas while the intimate dance club **Rouge** (180 Orchard Road, Peranakan Place Complex; tel: 6738 1000) has live rock music as well. **Ice Cold Beer** (9 Emerald Hill Road; tel: 6735 9929) serves beer straight from the tanks.

On the western end of Orchard Road are **Thumper** (Goodwood Park Hotel; tel: 6738 4867; <www.thumper.

New Asia Bar at the Swissôtel The Stamford

com.sg>), with 99 signature cocktails and an innovative biometric paying system; **Brix** (Grand Hyatt, 10 Scotts Road; tel: 6416 7292), with beautiful people and special theme nights; and the ever popular **Hard Rock Café** (02-01 HPL House, 50 Cuscaden Road; tel: 6235 5232; <www.hardrock.com>) has live music. All have cover charges that usually include one or two drinks.

Sentosa

Sentosa island has warmed up as an after-dark haunt with the entry of beachside clubs, which include the Ibizan import **Café del Mar** (40 Siloso Beach Walk; tel: 6235 1296; <www.cafedelmar.com.sg>) and the home-grown **Coastes** (50 Siloso Beach Walk; tel: 6274-9668; <www. coastes.com>), where you can enjoy cocktails and recline in a hammock.

Across Sentosa and next to VivoCity is **St James Power Station** (3 Sentosa Gateway; tel: 6270 7676; <www.stjames powerstation.com>), the largest party destination in town with nine different clubbing venues under one roof.

SPORTS

Singapore has fine facilities for sports activities. Active visitors should take heed of the high humidity and schedule outdoor workouts for early mornings or in the evenings.

Biking. Rentals are available at Sentosa, East Coast Park, Pasir Ris Park and Pulau Ubin.

Sea sports. Kayaking is available at Sentosa, East Coast Park and Changi Point while **cable skiing** is found at East Coast Lagoon (tel: 6442 7318; <www.ski360degree.com>). **Waterskiing** and **wakeboarding** are available at the Kallang River. **Windsurfing** equipment and small **sailboats** can be rented from the **SAFYC Sea Sports Centre** (11

Sailing at the East Coast

Changi Coast Walk; tel: 6546 5880).

Golf. Several of Singapore's golf courses are world class, attracting such international tournaments as the Johnnie Walker Classic. There are 11 private golf courses that offer limited access to non-members and four public courses that have no restrictions on visitors. Green fees range from S$40 for a nine-hole course on weekdays to S$400 for a full round at a championship course on weekends. Some clubs may ask you for a proficiency certificate. Clubs include **Changi Golf Club** (20 Netheravon Road; tel: 6545 5133; <www.changigolf club.org.sg>) with a nine-hole course and good views of the sea; **Orchid Country Club** (1 Orchid Club Road; tel: 6750 2111; <www.orchidclub.com>), which offers night golfing; the **Singapore Island Country Club** (180 Island Club Road; tel: 6459 2222; <www.sicc.org.sg>) with four 18-hole courses amidst the verdant MacRitchie Reservoir; **Sentosa Golf Club** (27 Bukit Manis Road, Sentosa Island; tel: 6275 0090; <www.sentosagolf.com>) with two of the most beautiful championship 18-hole courses in Singapore; and **Tanah Merah Country Club** (Changi Coast Road; tel: 6542 3040; <www.tmcc.org.sg>), which has two 18-hole courses.

Hiking. Despite the heat and humidity, hiking is certainly one of Singapore's most attractive outdoor pursuits. The **Bukit Timah Nature Reserve** (177 Hindhede Drive; tel: 6468 5736), **Sungei Buloh Wetland Reserve** (301 Neo Tiew Crescent; tel: 6794 1401; <www.sbwr.org.sg>; open Mon–Sat 7.30am–7pm, Sun 7am–7pm; free except Sat–Sun and public and school holidays) and **MacRitchie Nature Trail** (off Thomson Road at the Central Catchment Nature Reserve) are the three most popular trekking areas.

Spectator sports. Among the most popular are **cricket** and **rugby**, matches of which you might chance to see at the Padang across from the City Hall. The annual SCC International Rugby Sevens tournament (<www.sccrugbysevens.com>) is held here. Singapore also has its own **soccer** league (<www.sleague.com>), in which local and international teams compete at stadiums around the island. The **F1 Singapore Grand Prix** in September (tel: 6738 6738; <www.singaporegp.sg> is the first night race in F1 history (and Asia's first street race).

Horseracing. Live races can be enjoyed at the Singapore Turf Club (1 Turf Club Avenue, beside the Kranji MRT Station; tel: 6879 1000; <www.turfclub.com.sg>) on selected Friday nights and Saturday and Sunday afternoons.

Bikes are a great way to get around Sentosa

SINGAPORE FOR CHILDREN

Singapore has many attractions and entertainment options designed for visitors of all ages. Most offer child discounts.

With its beaches, oceanarium and theme parks, **Sentosa** *(see page 73)* is practically made for children. The **zoo** *(see page 69)* has a special area for younger children, and the **Night Safari** *(see page 71)* provides something exciting for families after nightfall. The **Jurong BirdPark** *(see page 66)* has highly entertaining shows.

The **Haw Par Villa** *(see page 64)* gives kids a chance to experience Chinese culture. The **Escape Theme Park** (1 Pasir Ris Close; open Sat–Sun, public and school holidays 10am–8pm; admission fee; tel: 6581 9112; <www.escapetheme park.com.sg>) is Singapore's largest theme park with more than a dozen rides. The **Singapore Discovery Centre** (510 Upper Jurong Road; open Tues–Sun 9am–6pm; admission fee; tel: 6792 6188; <www.sdc.com.sg>) is a high-tech edutainment attraction celebrating the history of Singapore. The **Singapore Science Centre** (15 Science Centre Road; open Tues–Sun 10am–6pm; admission fee; tel: 6425 2500; <www. science.edu.sg>) has over 850 exhibits, an aviation gallery and an Omni-theatre (open Tues–Sun 10am–8pm; admission fee). Nearby is **Snow City** (21 Jurong Town Hall Road; open Tues–Sun 9.45am–6.45pm, public and school holidays 9.45am–5.15pm; admission fee; tel: 6560 2306), where there is skiing and snowboarding indoors year round.

Escape Theme Park

Calendar of Events

Here is a list of the major festivals and events. Check exact dates with the Singapore Tourism Board (tel: 1800-736 2000; <www.visitsingapore.com>)

January/February *Chinese New Year:* lion dances, night bazaar and festival in Chinatown; *Chingay:* Orchard Road street parade with floats and stiltwalkers; *Thaipusam:* Hindu devotees carry metal structures *(kavadi)* on a 3-km (1¾-mile) pilgrimage of penance from Little India's Sri Srinivasa Perumal Temple to Sri Thandayuthapani (Chettiar) Temple in Tank Road.

March/April *Singapore International Film Festival:* foreign films and workshops; *World Gourmet Summit:* restaurants host international celebrity chefs.

May/June/July *Vesak Day:* birds released at temples to mark Buddha's entrance into Nirvana; *Singapore Dragon Boat Festival:* Chinese eat glutinous rice dumplings and join in dragon boat races to honour Qu Yuan, a patriotic martyr; *Great Singapore Sale:* huge discounts for eight weeks; *Singapore Arts Festival:* the best performing arts from the East and West; *Singapore Food Festival:* an annual gourmet splash in July.

August/September *Hungry Ghosts Festival:* spirits of the dead return in the 7th lunar month; with street banquets and Chinese operas; *National Day:* celebrates independence with a massive parade and fireworks; *F1 Singapore Grand Prix:* premier racing event; *Mooncake (Lantern) Festival:* traditional mid-autumn festivities in Chinatown and Chinese Garden.

October/November/December *Navarathiri Festival:* nine nights devoted to three Hindu goddesses, with music and procession at Sri Mariamman Temple; *Deepavali:* the Festival of Lights is celebrated in homes, Hindu temples and in the streets of Little India; *Thimithi Festival:* devotees walk over burning coals at the Sri Mariamman Temple; *Festival Light-Ups:* in Little India (Deepavali), Orchard Road (Christmas) and Geylang Serai (Hari Raya); *ZoukOut Dance Party:* international DJs spin from dusk to dawn.

Variable *Hari Raya Puasa:* Muslims celebrate the end of Ramadan (fasting month) with prayers, feasts and home visits; *Hari Raya Haji:* marks the sacrifices made by Muslims who undertake the *haj* (pilgrimage to Mecca).

EATING OUT

Singapore is one of the premier dining destinations in the world. The country is situated (geographically, historically and ethnically) on a culinary axis point where several of the world's top cuisines mix and mingle, from the great regional traditions of Chinese and Indian cooking to the more localised Malay and the Peranakan (Straits Chinese) cuisines. Thai, Indonesian, Japanese and Korean food is also amply represented, as is first-rate fare from the West. Eating out is also convenient, with good service and hygiene and English spoken. And meals, whether in fine-dining restaurants or hawker centres, are very affordable and of excellent value.

Be sure to sample each of Singapore's celebrated cuisines. Try out the various settings too, from hawker centres and quayside cafés to top hotel restaurants. Ask locals for tips, check out the latest local listings in the dailies and magazines, or buy a Singapore dining guide from a local bookstore.

For dinner, especially on weekends, reservations are a must at establishments that accept them. Otherwise, join the lines at the cafés, restaurants and food stalls. It is nearly always worth the wait.

Hawker Centres and Food Courts

Hawker centres are Singapore's answer to fast-food restaurants. Meals are very cheap, with main courses costing just a few dollars. Pictures of each dish often decorate a food hawker's counter, accompanied by names in English, making ordering a snap. Most offer a variety of freshly cooked Chinese, Malay and Indian choices. Your food is sometimes brought to your table (which you may have to share with others); other times you pick up your order on a tray. Singapore's most popular and crowded hawker centres are **Maxwell Food Centre**

Lau Pa Sat hawker centre

near Chinatown, **Newton Circus** across the Newton MRT Station and **Lau Pa Sat** near the Raffles Place MRT Station.

Food courts are slightly fancier than hawker centres, often located in shopping malls. These are air-conditioned, and prices are generally higher, but the same procedures apply.

Chinese Cuisine

The majority of Singaporeans are ethnically Chinese, so regional Chinese cuisines are amply represented. From Cantonese dim sum and Peking duck to Teochew rice porridge and Sichuan *mala* (spicy) hot pot steamboat, the choices offered by Chinese restaurants are endless.

Street-food-style offerings from Chinese hawkers are must tries. Offerings include *char kway teow* (fried rice noodles with clams, Chinese sausage and egg in a sweet black sauce), *popiah* (spring rolls with various fillings), wonton mee (minced meat dumpling and roast pork noodles) and *yong tau foo* (stuffed vegetables and bean curd, a Hakka speciality). Undoubtedly the single most popular dish is Hainanese chicken rice (pieces of chicken steamed in stock and served over boiled white rice with a chilli-ginger sauce), a staple at hawker centres, food courts and most Chinese coffee shops.

Malay Cuisine

Malay dishes tend to be spicy, with generous doses of lemongrass, chillies, cloves, tamarind and prawn paste. Coconut milk is also often added. For religious reasons, pork is never used.

A popular dish is *satay*, skewers of meat that are spiced and marinated before barbecuing. Satay, usually beef, mutton and chicken, is enjoyed with accompaniments such as *ketupat* (steamed rice wrapped in coconut leaves), cucumber, onions and a spicy peanut sauce. Two popular places to enjoy satay are **Clarke Quay** and **Boon Tat Street** next to Lau Pa Sat.

Spicy South Indian food

Among other savoury Malay offerings are *mee rebus* (yellow noodles in a thick spicy gravy), *gado gado* (vegetable salad smothered in a coconut and peanut sauce, served with prawn crackers), *nasi goreng* (fried rice), *soto ayam* (spicy chicken soup with rice cakes) and *rojak* (a sweet and spicy mix of pineapple, cucumber and fried bean curd with prawn paste and peanuts).

Peranakan (Nyonya) Cuisine

Nyonya (which refers to the women of a Peranakan or Straits-Chinese family of mixed Chinese and Malay heritage) cuisine is Singapore's most indigenous. Chinese and Malay ingredients and recipes have been transformed into some of Singapore's most delicious dishes. Peranakan restaurants proliferate in Katong in the eastern part of Singapore.

Coconut milk, shrimp paste *(belacan)* and chillies give Nyonya dishes a unique flavour. Shrimp paste, chilli and lime are pounded together to form a condiment called *sambal belacan*. Dishes worth trying are *buah keluak* (chicken and black nuts in tamarind sauce), *laksa* (noodles in curry sauce), *nyonya kueh* (glutinous rice cakes with coconut and sugar) and *otak-otak* (minced fish flavoured with lime and coconut, wrapped in banana leaves and charcoal roasted).

Indian Cuisine

The Indian food in Singapore is on par with the best dishes prepared in India itself. Diners are treated to the best of northern and southern Indian dishes, as well as creations that are uniquely Singaporean.

Northern Indian cuisine is mild and subtle, often employing yoghurt, wheat breads and ghee (clarified butter) rather than cooking oils. Tandoori (marinated meat or fish cooked in clay ovens) is the signature dish. In Singapore, the local variations on traditional northern Indian recipes have produced dishes like *mee goreng* (bean curd, mutton and peas fried with thick noodles in a tomato sauce) and *sup kambing* (a mutton soup accompanied by French bread).

Southern Indian cuisine is spicier and often less pricey. This is most often served in 'banana-leaf' restaurants, where a banana leaf replaces the plate. Rice is ladled onto the big leaf, followed by mounds of chutneys, dal (pureed lentils) and curries. The meal is eaten by hand, with the rice pinched between one's fingers. Vegetarians will enjoy southern Indian food as many dishes are meatless. Little India has a number of inexpensive vegetarian restaurants. Muslim Indian restaurants avoid pork but use other meats, especially in dishes such as *biryani*, which has a basmati-rice base.

Tea with the Queen

The perfect shopping and sightseeing break in bustling Singapore is a visit to a traditional Chinese teahouse. Singapore's best known is **Tea Chapter** (9/11 Neil Road; tel: 6226 1175; <www.tea-chapter.com.sg>), located near the Jinriksha Station). On 10 October 1989, Queen Elizabeth II and Prince Philip took their tea here in a private room upstairs overlooking the street. Visitors today can appreciate the pleasures of Chinese tea culture in the same room. The teas run the gamut, from greens to reds, but the service is traditional. Water is heated at the table, the tea arrives in tiny packets, and scoops, tea clips, fragrance cups, saucers and snacks complete the graceful setting.

Indian cooking is known for its delicious breads, ranging from the unleavened *chapati* to the fluffy *puri*. In Singapore, a popular bread is *roti prata*, a large, thin, folded pancake cooked on a hot griddle. When filled with spicy mutton (or chicken) and egg, it becomes *murtabak*, a staple at Indian street stalls and hawker centres.

Enjoy tea at a teahouse

Strangely enough, the best-known Indian dish in Singapore is not Indian at all, but rather a regional invention, the fish-head curry. The fish head is usually that of a red snapper, boiled in a spicy, complex curry and served eyeball-up.

Seafood

The alfresco seafood restaurants along East Coast Parkway do brisk business nearly every night, but it is difficult to tell if they are Chinese or simply Singaporean seafood restaurants. What's served is simply the fresh catch of the day, often perfectly prepared in any style you wish, with sauces of your choice. You can have squid deep fried, prawns in garlic and stingrays barbecued. Singapore's most popular signature seafood is chilli crab; pepper crab comes a close second. These are whole crabs stir fried with a fiery chilli or black pepper sauce.

Western Cuisine

French, Italian, European, Mediterranean, Middle Eastern and South American restaurants are scattered across Singapore. Top Western restaurants with foreign chefs are a staple in Sin-

A Singapore Sling from the Long Bar at the Raffles

gapore's international hotels, while finding an excellent French restaurant with a French chef at the helm in Singapore is easy. Fast-food chains, from Pizza Hut to McDonald's, are ubiquitous.

Some Singapore restaurants began combining Asian and Western ingredients and techniques even before the culinary revolution of the US West Coast. East–West fusion food, dubbed New Asian cuisine here, places great emphasis on the clever combination of Asian flavours with Continental methods of preparation and is well worth sampling at such establishments as Doc Cheng's at Raffles Hotel and Club Chinois at Orchard Parade Hotel.

Strange Fruits

Singapore's fresh-produce markets are the places to find all kinds of vegetables and fruits not normally seen in Western supermarkets. The most notorious is the durian, known as the king of fruits and well loved by most Singaporeans. Indeed, this spiny delight fetches royal prices, but to most foreigners, its smell is well beyond polite description. Public buildings and MRT stations in Singapore display signs prohibiting the durian's very presence.

Among fruits commonly found in Singapore are the rambutan (red and hairy in appearance), mangosteen (purple outside, white inside), *chiku* (brownish), starfruit (aptly named after its shape) and the red-and-white 'dragon fruit', whose mild taste is neither smoky nor fiery but similar to that of kiwi fruit.

Drinks and Desserts

Ginger tea, a staple of Indian drink vendors, is a strong contender to the lattes of Starbucks and other coffee chains. An even more direct contender is *kopi tarik*, the 'pulled coffee' that is 'pulled' by the maker from cup to pitcher and back again to ensure the ingredients are well mixed. Little India abounds with 'pulled-coffee' stalls. The same stunt is pulled to produce *teh tarik*, noted for its delicious froth.

In hawker centres and food courts, try freshly squeezed juices, or try a cold glass of soya bean milk or sugar cane juice with a wedge of lemon. The local beer is Tiger, a refreshing pilsner-style beer. Chinese teas are favoured by many Singaporean Chinese, served hot.

Refreshing local desserts, aimed at cooling the day's heat, include *cendol*, shaved ice and green jelly strips in coconut milk, and *ice kacang* (or *ais kacang*), shaved ice with red beans, jelly cubes, evaporated milk and coloured syrups.

Cookery Schools

Several culinary schools offer introductory courses to Asian cuisine, lasting from a day to several weeks. **At-sunrice** (Fort Canning Centre; tel. 6336 3307; <www.at-sunrice.com>) offers hands-on courses with a tour of an Asian spice garden. **The Raffles Culinary Academy** (02-17, Raffles Hotel Arcade, 1 Beach Road; tel. 6412 1256; <www.raffleshotel. com>) offers 4-hour classes Tues–Thur, where noted chefs demonstrate the preparation of regional dishes. **The Coriander Leaf** restaurant (3A Merchant Court, 02-03 River Valley Road, Clarke Quay; tel. 6732 3354; <www.corianderleaf.com>) has a studio teaching the preparation of Southeast Asian, Middle Eastern and fusion cuisines.

HANDY TRAVEL TIPS

An A–Z Summary of Practical Information

A Accommodation . . 107
Airport 107
B Budgeting for
Your Trip 108
C Car Hire 109
Climate 109
Clothing 110
Complaints 110
Crime and
Safety 111
Customs and Entry
Requirements . . 111
D Driving 112
E Electricity 114
Embassies and
Consulates 114
Emergencies 114
G Gay and Lesbian
Travellers 115
Getting There 115
Guides and Tours . 116

H Health and
Medical Care . . . 117
Holidays 117
I Internet 118
L Language 118
M Maps 119
Media 119
Money 120
O Opening Times . . . 120
P Post Offices 121
Public Transport . . 121
R Religion 123
T Telephone 123
Tickets 124
Time Zones 125
Tipping 125
Toilets 125
Tourist Information 125
W Water 127
Websites 127
Y Youth Hostels 127

ACCOMMODATION

There are hotels for every budget in Singapore. Major American and international hotel chains are well represented. Most hotels are concentrated in the Civic District (Raffles City, Marina Square areas), on or near Orchard Road and in Chinatown. The **Singapore Hotel Association**'s website, <www.stayinsingapore.com>, offers online hotel reservations. If you arrive without hotel reservations, the Singapore Hotel Association counters at the Changi Airport can arrange bookings. Pensions, hostels and bed and breakfast accommodation are few, but there are lots of budget hotels (many with air-conditioning). Travel agents, package travel services and travel web sites offer accommodation deals with substantial savings.

AIRPORT

Singapore Changi Airport (tel: 6542 1122; <www.changiairport. com.sg>) is frequently rated the best in the world. Disembarking passengers will discover why, as the march (assisted by travellators) through customs, immigration and baggage claim usually takes just a matter of minutes. There are three large terminals as well as a **Budget Terminal** (tel: 6412 7500; <www.btsingapore.com>) serving low-cost airlines. Clean, modern facilities include full-service banks, currency exchange counters, communication centres with telephone, fax, telegraph, copiers and internet access, post offices, free luggage trolleys, left luggage storage and duty-free shops. There are also hotel and car rental desks, nurseries, clinics, and restaurant and bar areas serving a range of international foods and drinks. Taxis, shuttle vans (Maxicabs) and city buses are available at terminal entrances (a 10-mile/16-km journey to downtown). Taxis cost about S$16 to S$24 for the ride dowtown (excluding surcharges) while the Maxicab costs S$7 per person. The MRT link from the airport to City Hall station downtown takes about half an hour and costs S$1.50.

Arrive two hours early for departing flights. Leaving Singapore, all passengers must pay an airport departure tax (S$21), which is usually incorporated into your air ticket these days. Transit passengers waiting a minimum of five hours may qualify for free city tours (check at the Singapore Visitors Centre in the Transit Hall). A transit hotel is available in the three terminals, renting rooms inexpensively in six-hour increments (tel: 6541 9106; <www.airport-hotel.com.sg>). Showers, saunas and gym facilities are also available for hire for travellers wishing to freshen up during a stopover. The airport and most facilities are open daily 7am–11pm. The flight information hotline (toll-free in Singapore only) is tel: 1800-542 4422.

B

BUDGETING FOR YOUR TRIP

Singapore has the second-highest standard of living in Asia (behind Japan), so expect many prices to be only slightly below those in North America and northern Europe. Food and transportation can be bargains. Meals at hawker centres and food courts can be as little as S$3. Subway (MRT) fares are between S$0.90 and S$1.90. City buses are just as cheap (S$0.90–1.80), and taxi trips around town are often as little as S$10. Hotels run the gamut, from under S$30 per person for budget choices to over S$500 for top accommodation. Private city tours are priced at S$28–100 and up.

Entrance fees to sights are reasonable (S$2–18), but entertainment costs (for performances, nightclubs, hotel night spots, bar and lounge drinks) can be as high as in Western capitals. Budget travellers can certainly visit Singapore cheaply. It is not a particularly expensive place, although Thailand, Malaysia, Indonesia and other nearby Southeast Asian destinations offer much lower prices on nearly everything. Singapore offers convenience, cleanliness, efficiency, superb meals and some great attractions, but it is not the bargain basement of Asia.

C

CAR HIRE

Car hire is seldom necessary in Singapore since it is compact and served by excellent and inexpensive forms of public transportation, but major car rental companies are in operation all over the island, including at the airport and downtown in the hotel districts. The Singapore government, in a concerted effort to reduce traffic congestion, has made car rental and use, especially in the central business district, an expensive and sometimes complicated affair. Rates for the smallest cars start at around S$150 per day (including insurance, CWD and unlimited mileage).

Rental cars can be taken into Malaysia, but surcharges and petrol restrictions apply (the tank must be at least three quarters full upon leaving Singapore). A valid driver's licence from your country of residence or a valid International Driving Licence is required, as is a major credit card. Some companies rent cars only to those over 21 and under 60. Petrol prices are higher in Singapore than in some European countries, and up to three times higher than in the US.

Major car rental companies in Singapore include:

Avis tel: 6737 1668; <www.avisworld.com>
Budget tel: 6532 4442; <www.budget.com>
Hertz tel: 1800-734 4646; <www.hertz.com>
National tel: 6737 1668; <www.nationalcar.com>

Avis and Hertz are the only car rental companies at the Singapore Changi Airport.

Hotels can often arrange for a car and driver; chauffeur-driven luxury cars can cost S$50 per hour and up.

CLIMATE

Singapore's tropical climate is fairly uniform, as are the hours of sunrise and sunset (6.30–7am/6.30–7pm), due to its location just 136 km (85 miles) north of the equator. Rainfall is heaviest from

November through January. Humidity is routinely very high all year round, averaging 80–85 percent. Daytime temperatures can soar near the average maximum of 31°C (88°F) in the afternoon and night-time lows can dip to near the average minimum of 24°C (75°F) just before sunrise. The lowest temperature ever recorded in Singapore was 19.4°C (68.9°F). Annual rainfall averages 2,337 mm (92 inches), with sudden but brief downpours common. For the weather forecast call tel: 6542 7788. Monthly average temperatures are as follows:

	J	F	M	A	M	J	J	A	S	O	N	D
°C	26	27	27	27	28	28	27	27	27	27	26	26
°F	79	81	81	81	82	82	81	81	81	81	79	79

CLOTHING

The island's dress code is casual but neat. Short-sleeved cotton sportswear is acceptable almost everywhere. Even businesspeople seldom wear suits or jackets. Some tourists wear shorts, as do many Singapore residents. Mosques require that arms and legs be fully covered (by long-sleeved shirts, long pants and long skirts or sarongs) to enter. Sikh temples require visitors to wear a head covering, as do synagogues for males. Raincoats are hardly necessary, although a light sweater or wrap is sometimes required in the evening and in air-conditioned indoors. Umbrellas are handy in a downpour. Hats and sunscreen can protect against the ravages of the fierce tropical sun. Comfortable walking shoes, sandals and sunglasses are useful for getting around.

COMPLAINTS

Report unsatisfactory retail practices to the **Singapore Tourism Board** (tel: 1800-736 2000). You can also contact the **Small Claims Tribunal** at the Subordinate Courts, 1st Floor, 1 Havelock Square (tel: 6435

5946; fax: 6435 5994; <www.smallclaims.gov.sg>), where complaints are heard on short notice and judgements are passed quickly.

CRIME AND SAFETY

Singapore has the lowest crime rate in Southeast Asia, but pick-pockets and purse snatchers do operate, usually around neighbourhood markets, even though the penalty for pickpocketing is three years in jail and four strokes of the cane. Crime is also very low in hotels, which have discreet security forces, but you are advised to use the hotel safety box or room safe for valuables. Report stolen property and other crimes immediately to your hotel and to the police (tel: 999 or 1800-225 0000).

Remember that Singapore has strict laws covering infractions that might be considered minor elsewhere. Littering can result in a S$1,000 fine for first-time offenders. Smoking is banned in public places, including restaurants and buses and taxis; the fine is S$1,000. The chewing of gum is not banned, but the unauthorised sale of chewing gum is subject to a S$2,000 fine.

Drug offences are dealt with harshly in Singapore. The death penalty is mandatory for those convicted of trafficking, manufacturing, importing or exporting 15g of heroin, 30g of cocaine, 30g of morphine, 500g of cannabis, 200g of cannabis resin, or 1.2kg of opium. Possession of these quantities is considered *prima facie* evidence of drug trafficking. Those convicted of drug consumption face a maximum prison term of 10 years and a fine of up to S$20,000. Singapore is definitely not the place to bring, buy, or use illegal drugs.

CUSTOMS AND ENTRY REQUIREMENTS

Citizens of Australia, New Zealand, South Africa, the United Kingdom, the Republic of Ireland, Canada and the US as well as of the Commonwealth, Western Europe and South America need only a valid passport (good for six months) to enter Singapore for a tourist or business visit lasting up to 30 days. Tourists, however, should also carry onward/return tickets to their next destination and sufficient funds for their stay in Singapore. For longer stays, apply to the **Immigration & Checkpoints Authority (ICA)** office (10 Kallang Road; <www.ica.gov.sg>) or call the hotline (tel: 6391 6100) upon arrival. Vaccination certificates are required only of passengers who arrive from cholera- or yellow fever-infected areas. An immigration card, supplied before arrival, must be filled out and kept with the passport for surrender upon departure.

Visitors carrying more than the equivalent of S$30,000 in cash or cheque have to report this fact to the customs authorities. Customs limitations for personal consumption apply to certain items, including spirits (1 litre), wine or port (1 litre) and beer, stout or ale (1 litre). There are no concessions on cigarettes and other tobacco products (in line with the government's campaign to discourage smoking). Travellers with medicines must bring prescriptions authorising their use. Prohibited items include controlled drugs and psychotropic substances, weapons, ammunition, endangered species and their by-products, firecrackers, seditious and treasonable materials and obscene (pornographic) articles, publications, video tapes and software. A complete list of prohibited, restricted and dutiable goods is available from the Customs Duty Officer, Singapore Changi Airport (tel: 6542 7058 or 6543 0755; <www.customs.gov.sg>).

Lost or stolen passports should be reported to the police, then to ICA (tel: 6391 6100), where temporary passports are issued, and finally to your embassy.

D

DRIVING

Motorists drive on the left, overtake on the right and fully yield to pedestrians at designated crossing points. A valid driver's licence or an International Driving Licence is required. Speed limits are 50–60 km/h (30–37 mph) in residential areas, 70–90 km/h (40–50 mph) on expressways. Singapore roads are in excellent condition and sign-posted in English. Speed cameras are installed throughout the island. Bus lanes or lanes with unbroken yellow lines are used only by buses during rush hours (Mon–Fri 7.30–9.30am and 5–8pm). Full-day bus lanes (Mon–Sat 7.30am–8pm) are marked by red lines and run along Orchard Road, Eu Tong Sen Street, Hill Street, Victoria Street, Bras Basah Road and Somerset Road.

All vehicles entering the Central Business District (CBD) from 7.30am to 7pm from Monday to Friday are required to pay an Electronic Road Pricing (ERP) toll. ERP tolls are also levied on expressways during peak hours (check details with the **Land Transport Authority**, tel:1800-225 5582; <www.lta.gov.sg>). All vehicles are installed with an In-Vehicle Unit (IU) and a cash card (stored-value card). The toll is automatically deducted from the cash card each time the vehicle passes through an ERP gantry. The toll varies with the time of day and entry point. The ERP is not in operation on Sunday and public holidays. There are tolls for using the Causeway and Second Link bridges that connect Singapore and Malaysia.

Driving information is available from the **Automobile Association of Singapore** (AAS; tel: 6333 8811; <www.aas.com.sg>) and the Land Transport Authority (tel: 1800-225 5582; <www.lta.gov.sg>). The AAS emergency road service operates 24 hours a day (tel: 6748 9911). The traffic police can be contacted at tel: 1800-547 1818.

At public car parks and for on-street parking, a pre-paid parking coupon must be displayed indicating the date and the time of arrival. These parking coupons are sold at petrol stations, post offices and convenience stores. In the car parks of most shopping centres and public buildings, cash card payment is used. Depending on the system installed, you will need to insert your cash card either into a machine at the entrance or into your car's IU so the fee can be deducted when you pass through the gantry.

Petrol is sold by the litre (one US gallon equals 3.8 litres; one imperial gallon equals 4.5 litres).

E

ELECTRICITY

Singapore's voltage is 220–240 A.C., 50 Hertz. Most hotels provide a transformer to convert to 110–120 A.C., 60 Hertz. Outlets require plugs with two round large prongs or the three-pronged square type.

EMBASSIES, CONSULATES AND HIGH COMMISSIONS

Foreign missions and embassies are generally open Monday to Friday, 9am to 5pm, although some work shorter hours.

Australia: High Commission, 25 Napier Road, tel: 6836 4100; <www.singapore.embassy.gov.au>
Canada: High Commission, 11-01, 1 George Street, tel: 6854 5900; <geo.international.gc.ca/asia/singapore>
New Zealand: High Commission, 15-06/10 Ngee Ann City Tower A, 391A Orchard Road, tel: 6235 9966; <www.nzembassy.com>
UK: High Commission, 100 Tanglin Road, tel: 6424 4200; <www.britain.org.sg>
France: Embassy, 101–103 Cluny Park Road, tel: 6880 7800; <www.ambafrance-sg.org>
Germany: Embassy, 12-00 Singapore Land Tower, 50 Raffles Place, tel: 6533 6002; <www.singapur.diplo.de>
US: Embassy, 27 Napier Road, tel: 6476 9100; <singapore.us embassy.gov>

EMERGENCIES

If you are in a hotel, call the front desk, operator or hotel security. General emergency telephone numbers are:

Police	**999**
Ambulance	**995**
Fire	**995**
24-hour Touristline	**1800-736 2000**

G

GAY AND LESBIAN TRAVELLERS

Homosexual activity is illegal in Singapore. This said, there is a discreet homosexual scene and a few gay-friendly entertainment venues, mainly in Tanjong Pagar and the Chinatown area.

GETTING THERE

By air. Singapore is served by about 80 international airlines, representing more than 56 countries. As a major Asian hub, the Singapore Changi Airport is a superb stopover. Relatively inexpensive air tickets to nearby countries can be purchased through hundreds of travel agents in Singapore. Tickets during the high season (June to September and December to January, from Europe and North America; December to January from Australia and New Zealand) are the most expensive.

Singapore Airlines, the national air carrier, is frequently rated the world's best airline. It offers non-stop and one-stop flights to and from many cities, including Vancouver in Canada; Los Angeles, San Francisco, New York and Chicago in the US; Adelaide, Brisbane, Melbourne, Perth and Sydney in Australia; Auckland and Christchurch in New Zealand; London and Manchester in the UK; and Durban and Johannesburg in South Africa. Singapore Airlines has offices in all the countries it serves, including the United States (tel: 800-742 3333), the United Kingdom (tel: 208-750 2708), Canada (tel: 800-663 3046), Ireland (tel: 01-671 0722), Australia (tel: 02-9350 0100), New Zealand (tel: 09-379 3209), South Africa (tel: 011-880 8560) and in Singapore itself (02-38/39 The Paragon, 290 Orchard Road; tel: 6223 8888; <www.singaporeair.com.sg>). Singapore Airlines provides for early check-in (up to 48 hours in advance) at its Singapore office or over the Internet. Singapore is also home to budget airlines Tiger Airways (tel: 6538 4437; <www.tigerairways.com>) and Jetstar Asia (tel: 6822 2288; <www.jetstar.com/sg>).

By rail. Visitors can also enter and leave Singapore via bus or rail through Malaysia. Five trains a day, all operated by **Keretapi Tanah Melayu Berhad (KTMB)** (tel: 6222 5165 in Singapore; <www.ktmb.com.my>), connect Singapore to Kuala Lumpur and other west coast and central Malaysian cities. A daily International Express Train connects Singapore to Thailand, as does the upscale **Eastern & Orient Express** (tel: 6392 3500 in Singapore, 800-524 2420 in US; <www.orient-express.com>), which takes 50 hours to make the Bangkok–Singapore run. The Tanjong Pagar Railway Station (tel: 6222 5165) is on Keppel Road, a 20-minute walk from the Tanjong Pagar MRT station.

GUIDES AND TOURS

Various private and group tours are offered by Singapore tour companies. These can be booked directly or through hotel tour desks. Use guides licensed and trained by the Singapore Tourism Board (STB). There are city tours, historic tours, tours geared to specific attractions, evening tours and harbour and river tours, as well as specialised tours focusing on food, farming, Chinese opera, *feng shui* (Chinese geomancy) and horseracing. Leading tour operators include the award-winning **Holiday Tours** (tel: 6738 2622) and **RMG Tours** (tel: 6220 8722; <www.rmgtours.com>). The zany **DUCK Tours** (tel: 6338 6877; <www.ducktours.com.sg>) take you from land to river as they cover key tourist sights in their amphibious half-boat, half-truck vehicles. The same company also offers **HiPPOtours**, which are city sightseeing trips on open-top double-decker bus. Visitors can hop on and off at designated stops along the way. Journeys (tel: 6325 1631; <www.singaporewalks.com>) offer the **Original Singapore Walks**, which take you to the more unusual places of interest, including 'wet' markets, red-light districts, 'haunted' nooks and graveyards. If it's private taxi tours you prefer, qualified **taxi-cum-tourist guides** are available: call CityCab (tel: 6542 5831/6542 8297; <www.citycab.com.sg>), Comfort (tel: 9181 7011; <www.comfort-transportation.com.sg>), or SMRT (tel: 6555 8888; <www.smrt.com.sg>) to arrange.

H

HEALTH AND MEDICAL CARE

Singapore has no free medical care and medical evacuation is very expensive, so be sure you are covered by your travel insurance. Most hotels have doctors on call around the clock. Singapore's medical facilities are the finest in Asia. The **Raffles Medical Clinic** (585 North Bridge Road, tel: 6311 1555; <www.rafflesmedical.com>) is a 24-hour clinic and the **Singapore General Hospital** on Outram Road (tel: 6222 3322 or 1800-223 0118; <www.sgh.com.sg>) is also always open. For ambulance service, dial 995. Pharmacies are open 9am to 6pm, sometimes later, but it is wise to travel with your own prescriptions and medications. Drink plenty of liquids to avoid heat exhaustion and use sunscreen.

HOLIDAYS

The following are national holidays. Banks and government offices are closed on these dates, as are some shops. When a public holiday falls on a Sunday, the following Monday is usually a national holiday.

New Year's Day	1 January
Chinese New Year	The first two days of the first lunar month; usually in January or February.
Hari Raya Haji	Muslim pilgrimage celebrations; date changes annually.
Good Friday	Usually in March or April.
Labour Day	1 May
Vesak Day	Buddha's birthday; 8th day of the 4th lunar month, usually in May or June.
National Day	9 August
Deepavali	Hindu festival; usually in October/November
Hari Raya Puasa	Last day of Ramadan, 9th month of the Islamic calendar; date changes annually.
Christmas	25 December

INTERNET

To get online, head to an internet café (try **Chills Café** at 39 Stamford Road, 01-07; tel: 6883 1016; <www.chillscafe.com.sg>; open daily 9am–midnight) or public libraries which offer cheap internet access.

Alternatively, **Wireless@SG** is a new system that provides free wireless connection at selected hot spots around Singapore. Visitors will need a mobile device with WiFi facility, and will have to register with one of the three service providers: iCELL Network (tel: 6773 4284; <www.icellnetwork.com>), QMax Communications (tel: 6796 0313; <www.qmax.com.sg>) and Singapore Telecommunications (tel: 1610; <www.singtel.com>). Check the Infocomm Development Authority website <www.ida.gov.sg> for an updated list of hot spots.

LANGUAGE

Singapore has four official languages: English (the language of administration), Chinese (Mandarin), Tamil and Malay. English is widely spoken. Malay, designated as the national language, is spoken by only 15 percent of the population but understood by many Singaporeans. Mandarin Chinese is being pushed by the government as the preferred Chinese language, but Singapore's ethnic Chinese majority speaks one or more of the southern languages as well, mainly Hokkien, Teochew, Cantonese and Hainanese. Singapore's ethnic Indians speak Tamil but many also speak Telugu, Punjabi, Hindi, Bengali and other regional languages. English serves as the island's lingua franca, although the government is attempting to discourage the use of a widespread local form of pidgin known as Singlish, or Singaporean English.

M

MAPS

Free city maps are available at Changi Airport's arrival hall, most hotels and at Singapore Tourism Board's visitor centres *(see page 126)*. The free monthly *The Official Guide & Map* and *Where Singapore* magazine also contain maps.

Most bookshops also stock maps of Singapore. A good one to get is the **Insight Fleximap Singapore**, laminated for durability and easy folding.

MEDIA

Of the nine major daily newspapers published in Singapore, four are in English, led by *The Straits Times*, which covers local, regional and international news. *The Edge Singapore* is a business and investment weekly. Local magazines in English include *I–S*, *Time Out*, *Where Singapore* and *8 Days*, all of which cover entertainment, attractions and shopping. *Wine and Dine* concentrates on dining. International newspapers and magazines are available at bookstores, newsstands, shopping centres and hotel kiosks. Some publications are subject to government-controlled circulation quotas. Magazines such as *Playboy* are banned, as are any publications with articles deemed harmful or offensive to Singapore.

Cable and satellite TV broadcasts, with CNN, BBC, MTV, NHK, ESPN and other common channels, are widely available in hotels. Local TV stations broadcast via the following channels: Channel 5 in English, Channel 8 and Channel U in Chinese; Suria in Malay; Central shows Tamil, arts and documentary programmes; and Channel NewsAsia broadcasts news and current affairs programmes. Two stations from Malaysia are also received in Singapore.

Eight of the local radio stations broadcast in English. BBC World Service is also available on FM radio.

MONEY

Currency. The Singapore dollar (abbreviated S$ or SGD) is divided into 100 cents, with coins of 1, 5, 10, 20, 50 cents and S$1. Bills in common circulation are S$2, S$5, S$10, S$20, S$50, S$100, S$500, S$1,000 and S$10,000.

Currency exchange. Money-changing services are available at the Changi Airport and at most banks, hotels and shopping complexes. Licensed money changers (usually located in popular shopping malls) mostly give slightly better rates than banks; hotels give the worst rates. The exchange rates at the airport are on par with those at downtown banks.

Credit cards. Major credit cards are widely accepted by Singapore's restaurants, hotels, shops, travel agencies and taxis.

Traveller's cheques. Traveller's cheques are easy to exchange for local currency and are accepted at many stores, restaurants and hotels.

Report lost or stolen credit cards immediately to the police (tel: 1800-353 0000). In Singapore, you can call American Express (tel: 1800-737 8188), Diners Club (tel: 6416 0800/0900), Mastercard (tel: 800-110 0113) and Visa (tel: 800-448 1250) for replacements.

ATMs. Automated teller machines are everywhere (at banks, shopping malls and many hotels). The Cirrus and PLUS system machines work in Singapore just as they do overseas.

OPENING TIMES

Museums and tourist attractions have varying hours, but many open at about 9.30am and close at 5 or 6pm; some are closed at least one day a week. Banks are usually open Monday to Friday 9.30am to

3pm, Saturdays 9.30am to 12.30pm (but Saturday hours can vary). Government offices operate Monday to Friday 8am to 6pm; some are open on Saturday. Many restaurants are open daily from 11.30am to 10pm, but most hawker centres keep long hours, from dawn to midnight daily. Department stores and shopping centres are generally open daily from 10am to 9pm.

P

POST OFFICES

Letters and postcards can be dropped off at hotel front desks, which often sell postage. Branches of the **Singapore Post** are generally open Monday to Friday 8.30am to 5pm and Saturday till 1pm. The Singapore Post branch at 04-15 Takashimaya, Ngee Ann City, 391 Orchard Road (tel: 6738 6899) is open Monday to Friday 9.30am to 6.30pm, Saturday 9.30am to 3pm. The Changi Airport Post Office is open daily 8am to 9.30pm at Terminal 2 Departure Hall, and open daily 6am–midnight at Terminal 2 Transit. For post office inquiries and locations, dial 1605. DHL, FedEx, TNT and UPS provide courier services as well.

PUBLIC TRANSPORT

Buses. Singapore has an efficient public bus system. Fares are S$0.80 to S$1.50 for non-air-conditioned buses, S$0.90 to S$1.80 for air-conditioned buses. Buses operate daily from 6am to midnight. Ask the driver for the fare to your destination; exact change is required and the money is deposited into a box near the driver.

Alternatively, purchase the **Singapore Tourist Pass** (www.singaporetouristpass.com) at selected MRT stations. Enjoy unlimited rides on buses and trains for just S$8 a day. Also available are 2-day (S$16) and 3-day (S$24) passes. To use the card, either flash or tap it on the electronic readers mounted at bus entrances and entry turnstiles of MRT stations. If you are planning to be in

Singapore for a longer period, buy an **ez-link card** (stored-value transportation card). An ez-link card costs a minimum of S$15 (including a $5 non-refundable deposit), and can be purchased at all TransitLink offices at MRT stations and bus interchanges. A helpful source for information is the "Travel with Ease" Public Transport Guide for Tourists, available at Singapore Visitors Centres and MRT stations.

NightRider. Night buses run from 11.30pm to 4.30am on Friday, Saturday and eves of public holidays. Trips cost a flat fee of S$3. They provide an inexpensive way of getting around late at night. The routes pass major nightlife areas, including Boat Quay, Clarke Quay, Mohamed Sultan and Orchard Road. Check <www.smrt buses.com.sg/transport/bus/NightRider> for detailed routes.

SIA Hop-On by SH Tours (tel: 6734 9923; <www.asiatours.com.sg>) is a tourist bus service that plys the major landmarks and attractions around the city area. As its name implies, you hop on (and off) as you wish along various designated stops. One-day tickets are S$3 for Singapore Airlines and SilkAir passengers visiting Singapore and S$12 (adult), S$6 (child) for other passengers.

Subway (MRT). Singapore's Mass Rapid Transit (MRT) system is very efficient and simple to use. It operates from 5.15am to 12.50am daily, with trains arriving every 3 to 8 minutes. Single trip tickets start at S$0.90, in addition to a S$1 refundable deposit. Because this can prove quite cumbersome, it makes more sense to get the Singapore Tourist Pass or an ez-link fare card *(see above)* even if you're just visiting the country for a day. Rush hours should be avoided. For information, call tel: 1800-225 5663, daily 8am–6pm. There are three MRT lines, the East-West, North-South and Northeast lines. The network will become more extensive with the completion of the round-island Circle Line by 2010.

Trishaws. These pedal-driven carts can make for an interesting tour, but be sure to agree on the full fare before boarding. Some tour operators offer city tours by trishaw.

Taxis. Singapore's 23,000 taxis are air-conditioned, comfortable and highly efficient. Most of the drivers are exceptionally friendly and helpful, although a few can be a bit gruff. Within the CBD (including Orchard Road) taxis can only be boarded and alighted at taxi stands and along side roads; elsewhere in Singapore, simply flag one along the road. All taxis are metered; most accept credit cards. Basic fares are S$2.80–3.20 for the first km, S$0.20 for each 385 m (421 yds) thereafter, with extra charges for waiting time. A variety of surcharges are thrown in for midnight to 6am trips (50 percent is added to the meter fare), peak period travel, travel into restricted downtown zones, advanced booking and airport travel. The three major taxi companies are CityCab (tel: 6552 2222), Comfort (tel: 6552 1111) and SMRT (tel: 6555 8888).

R

RELIGION

Singapore's major religions are Buddhism (42.5 percent), Islam (14.9 percent), Christianity (14.6 percent), Taoism (8.5 percent) and Hinduism (4.0 percent). Other religions, including Judaism, account for 0.6 percent, with 14.8 percent of the population reporting no religious affiliation. Nearly every Christian denomination has a church in Singapore.

T

TELEPHONE

The country code for Singapore is 65. International calls to Singapore are made by dialling the international access code for the originating country, followed by Singapore's country code and the eight-digit local number. International calls from Singapore are made by dialling the international access code (001, 013 or 019) followed by the country code, area code and local number.

Most telephones in Singapore operate using phone cards (stored value cards), which can be purchased from all post offices and be used for making local and overseas calls. International calling cards can be used from any phone; simply dial the calling card's access number for Singapore and follow the instructions.

Local calls in Singapore made from from public phones cost S$0.10 for the first 3 minutes and S$0.10 for every subsequent 3 minutes, up to a maximum of 9 minutes. No area codes are used within Singapore. Dial 100 for local call assistance; dial 104 for overseas call assistance.

Mobile phones. Only users of GSM mobile phones with global roaming service can connect automatically with Singapore's phone networks. If you are planning to be in Singapore for any length of time, it may be more economical to buy a local SIM card from one of the three service providers: Singtel (tel: 1626 or 6738 0123), M1 (tel: 1627 or 1800-843 8383) or Starhub (tel: 1633 or 6820 1633). These cards give you a local mobile number and cost a minimum of S$20.

Note: All local mobile numbers begin with '8' or '9'.

TICKETS

Tickets for performing arts and athletic events can be booked by phone, in person and online (and paid for in all cases by credit card) with two ticketing providers: **SISTIC** (tel: 6348 5555; <www.sistic.com.sg>) or **tickets.com** (tel: 6296 2929; <www.tdc.sg>). SISTIC outlets are located at 1 Temasek Avenue (Millenia Walk), 252 North Bridge Road (Raffles City Shopping Centre) and 435 Orchard Road (Wisma Atria), while tickets.com outlets are located at 176 Orchard Road (Centrepoint) and 163 Tanglin Road (Tanglin Mall).

TIME ZONES

Singapore time is GMT +8 hours year round. Thus, in the winter, when it is 6pm in Singapore it is 2am (16 hours earlier) in Los Angeles and Vancouver, 5am (13 hours earlier) in New York and Toronto, 10am (8 hours earlier) in London and Dublin, noon (6 hours earlier) in Johannesburg, 8pm (2 hours later) in Sydney and 10pm (4 hours later) in Auckland. Although the clock is advanced one hour in summer in some countries (such as the US), it stays the same in Singapore.

For the time of day in Singapore and world time, tel: 1711.

TIPPING

Tipping is usually not practised in Singapore. It is not allowed at the Changi Airport and discouraged in many hotels and restaurants, where a 10 percent service charge is routinely added to bills on top of the Goods and Services Tax (GST) of 7 percent. Tour guides and drivers do appreciate tips (5 to 10 percent). Very small tips (S$1–2) can be paid to taxi drivers, porters and hotel housekeeping staff.

TOILETS

Singapore's public restrooms are reasonably clean and are regularly inspected by health department officials. Most are free, but there's sometimes a nominal charge (S$0.10–S$0.20) for their use.

TOURIST INFORMATION

The **Singapore Tourism Board** (STB) is a superb organisation, offering mountains of free and helpful literature to visitors. Their website is <www.visitsingapore.com>.

STB offices abroad include the following:

Australia: Level 11, AWA Building, 47 York Street, Sydney NSW 2000; tel: 02-9290 2888 or 9290 2882; fax: 02-9290 2555; email: <stb-syd@stb-syd.org.au>

Germany: Hochstrasse 35–37, 60313 Frankfurt am Main; tel: 069-920 77018; fax: 069-297 8922; email: <info@stb-germany.de>

New Zealand: Representative Office, c/o Vivaldi World Limited, 1340-C Glenbrook Road RD1, Waiuku, Auckland; tel: 800-608 506; fax: 09- 290 2555; email: <stbnz@stb-syd.org.au>

UK: Singapore Centre, Grand Buildings, 1–3 Strand, London WC2N 5HR; tel: 020-7484 2710; fax: 020-7839 6162; email: <stb_london@stb.gov.sg>

US: Los Angeles: 5670 Wilshire Boulevard, 1550 Los Angeles, CA 90036; tel: 323-677-0808; fax: 323-677 0801; email: <losangeles@stb.gov.sg>

New York: 1156 Avenue of the Americas, Suite 702, New York, NY 10036; tel: 212-302 4861; fax: 212-302 4801; email: <new york@stb.gov.sg>

The Singapore Tourism Board runs a 24-hour tourist information hotline: 1800-736 2000 (toll-free in Singapore), 65-6736 2000 (from overseas). Visitor centres are at the following locations:

Singapore Changi Airport Transit Halls: Arrival Halls and Transit Halls, Terminals 1, 2 and 3; open daily 6am–2am

Junction of Cairnhill and Orchard Road: open daily 9.30am–10.30pm

Suntec City Mall: 01-35, The Galleria@Suntec City Mall, 3 Temasek Boulevard; open daily 10am–6pm

Liang Court: Level 1, 177 River Valley Road; open daily 10am–10pm

Cruise Centre: 01-31D Arrival Hall, HarbourFront Centre, 1 Maritime Square; open daily 24 hours

Inncrowd Backpackers' Hostel: Little India, 73 Dunlop Street; open daily 10am–10pm

W

WATER

Due to its limited natural resources, Singapore has long depended on neighbouring Malaysia for most of its water supply. In an effort to be more self-sufficient, since February 2003, Singaporeans have slowly been getting used to Newater, a catchword for reclaimed water which has been put through a rigorous purification process. Only a trickle of Newater is mixed into reservoir water currently – just 1 percent of the 300 million gallons consumed daily. By 2011 the proportion is targeted to increase to about 2.5 percent. Despite this, tap water is perfectly safe to drink in Singapore. Bottled water (local and international brands) is widely available.

WEBSITES

The internet provides many sites for information about Singapore.
<www.changiairport.com.sg> Changi Airport
<www.stayinsingapore.com> Online hotel bookings
<www.visitsingapore.com> Singapore Tourism Board (STB)
<www.gov.sg> Official Singapore government site
<www.makansutra.com> Details the best hawker fare
<www.wineanddine.asiaone.com.sg> Food reviews and listings

Y

YOUTH HOSTELS

There are a few Hostelling International (HI) accommodation in Singapore, namely the **Costa Sands resorts** at Pasir Ris, Downtown East and Sentosa, and **Hangout@Mt Emily**. Check <www.hisingapore.org.sg> for details. A few other inexpensive accommodation also offer dorms and small rooms with shared baths, such as the **Fort Canning Lodge YWCA** and the **YMCA** on Orchard Road *(pages 130 and 134)*.

Recommended Hotels

Singapore has several of the world's top-rated luxury hotels, a number of new boutique hotels, and some of the cleanest budget rooms in Asia.

Posted hotel prices tend to be fairly expensive, but hefty discounts are common. Occupancy is at its highest during the high season (August and December to the end of Chinese New Year) and reservations are recommended. You can book a room yourself on the Singapore Hotel Association's website <www.stayinsingapore.com>, which includes full descriptions, rates, and specials for nearly every hotel and inn in Singapore.

All accommodation accept major credit cards, except where noted. Meals are normally not included, although some hotels and resorts have package specials that include buffet breakfasts.

Each entry is marked with a symbol indicating the approximate room rate charged per night for a double room with bathroom. Prices do not include the 10 percent service charge and 7 percent goods and services tax, except where noted.

$$$$$	S$350 and more
$$$$	S$250–350
$$$	S$150–250
$$	S$80–150
$	up to S$80

SINGAPORE RIVER

Conrad Centennial $$$$$ *2 Temasek Boulevard, Singapore 038982; tel: 6334 8888; fax: 6333 9166; <www.conradhotels. com>.* Adjacent to Suntec City, this hotel has large rooms, marble-clad bathrooms, top services and an outdoor pool. Disabled access. 509 rooms.

The Fullerton $$$$$ *1 Fullerton Square, Singapore 049178; tel: 6733 8388; fax: 6735 8388; <www.fullertonhotel.com>.* Created within a 1928 colonial landmark fronting Marina Bay, the

Fullerton is aiming to become Asia's top hotel, with grand facilities and services as well as acclaimed bars and restaurants to match. Business travellers will appreciate its proximity to the financial district. Disabled access. 400 rooms.

The Gallery Hotel $$$ *1 Nanson Road, Singapore 238909; tel: 6849 8686; fax: 6836 6666; <www.galleryhotel.com.sg>.* With its postmodernist architecture and compact rooms and suites artfully decorated by young artists, this is definitely a hotel for design-conscious visitors. Many rooms overlook the Singapore River. Free Internet access is provided in every room. Disabled access. 223 rooms.

Grand Copthorne Waterfront $$$–$$$$ *392 Havelock Road, Singapore 169663; tel: 6733 0880; fax: 6737 8880; <www. millenniumhotels.com>.* A luxury hotel located right on the Singapore River, the Grand Copthorne has a marvellous riverside ambience and alfresco dining. Disabled access. 538 rooms.

Novotel Clarke Quay Singapore $$$–$$$$ *177A River Valley Road, Singapore 179031; tel: 6338 3333; fax: 6339 2854; <www. novotel.com>.* Located beside the Singapore River, the Novotel Clarke Quay has modern rooms with private balconies. It also offers organised walking tours and boat excursions. 402 rooms.

Pan Pacific $$$$ *7 Raffles Boulevard, Marina Square, Singapore 039595; tel: 6336 8111; fax: 6339 1861; <www.pan pacific.com>.* Marina Bay's most spacious modern hotel is quite luxurious, offering spectacular harbour views and a 35-storey-high atrium that's touted to be the highest in Southeast Asia. 775 rooms.

The Ritz-Carlton, Millenia $$$$$ *7 Raffles Avenue, Singapore 039799; tel: 6337 8888; fax: 6338 0001; <www.ritzcarlton.com>.* This luxury hotel at Marina Bay has larger-than-average rooms and stunning bathrooms. It has an impressive contemporary art collection, and its 32-storey tower overlooks the harbour, the city and Millenia Walk shopping mall. Disabled access. 608 rooms.

Fort Canning Lodge YWCA $$ *6 Fort Canning Road, Singapore 179494; tel: 6338 4222; fax: 6337 4222; <www.ywcaflodge.org. sg>.* Located on peaceful Fort Canning Hill, the YWCA has dorms and rooms, some with private baths, for single women, couples and families. A short walk to attractions and Orchard Road. 175 rooms.

Grand Plaza Park Hotel City Hall $$–$$$ *10 Coleman Street, Singapore 179809; tel: 6336 3456; fax: 6339 9311; <www.parkhotel group.com>.* This luxury business hotel is located close to popular tourist sights and major shopping malls. It has an excellent spa, the marine-themed St Gregory Spa. Disabled access. 326 rooms.

Hangout@Mt Emily $–$$ *10A Upper Wilkie Road, Singapore 228119; tel: 6438 5588; fax: 6339 6008; <www.hangouthotels. com>.* An inexpensive, fun and comfortable hostel that knows just what budget travellers want. This Hostelling International (HI) hostel offers 24-hour free Internet access and warm and friendly service. 61 rooms with ensuites and 25 dorm beds.

InterContinental $$$$ *80 Middle Road, Singapore 188966; tel: 6338 7600; fax: 6338 7366; <singapore.intercontinental.com>.* Adjoining the air-conditioned shopping mall Parco Bugis Junction that is built over restored pre-war shophouses, this award-winning luxury tower offers shophouse-themed rooms with Peranakan artefacts. Disabled access. 403 rooms.

Raffles Hotel $$$$$ *1 Beach Road, Singapore 189673; tel: 6337 1886; fax: 6339 7650; <www.raffleshotel.com>.* The Raffles is one of the legendary hotels of Asia. Restored to an all-suites hotel, this national monument is thoroughly plush, worthy of Singapore's highest room rates. Its Long Bar is famous as the place where the Singapore Sling cocktail was first concocted. Disabled access. 103 rooms.

Swissôtel The Stamford $$$$ *2 Stamford Road, Singapore 178882; tel: 6338 8585; fax: 6338 2862; <www.singapore-stamford. swissotel.com>.* This hotel is located near the CBD and is practically part of a large shopping complex. Business centre, convention centre and a huge number of restaurants and bars (including the excellent rooftop Equinox complex), plus a luxurious spa and a well-equipped fitness centre. Disabled access. 1,261 rooms.

CHINATOWN

Berjaya Hotel $$$ *83 Duxton Road, Singapore 089540; tel: 6227 7678; fax: 6227 1232; <www.berjayaresorts.com>.* One of Chinatown's most elegant boutique hotels, the Berjaya decorates its rooms with colonial and Straits Chinese furnishings. This is located close to the business district and has an Italian-Mediterranean fine-dining restaurant. 48 rooms.

Hotel 1929 $$$ *50 Keong Saik Road, Singapore 089154; tel: 6347 1929; fax: 6327 1929; <www.hotel1929.com>.* This boutique property combines a mix of old-world Singapore architecture and nouveau-chic style. No two rooms are designed the same way and many are embellished with unique furniture from the owner's private collection. Its Ember restaurant has won rave reviews for its chic ambience and creative fusion cuisine. 32 rooms.

New Majestic Hotel $$$ *31–37 Bukit Pasoh Road, Singapore 089845; tel: 6511 4700; fax: 6227 3301; <www.newmajestichotel. com>.* This hot boutique hotel oozes style and individuality from all corners, from the custom-designed rooms done up by some of Singapore's brightest young artists to its acclaimed modern Chinese restaurant. 30 rooms.

The Scarlet $$–$$$ *33 Erskine Road, Singapore 069333; tel: 6511 3333; fax: 6511 3303; <www.thescarlethotel.com>.* Located near Chinatown, this boutique hotel is luxurious and dramatic, with characterful ensuite rooms. 84 rooms.

LITTLE INDIA

Albert Court $$–$$$ *180 Albert Street, Singapore 189971; tel: 6339 3939; fax: 6339 3253; <www.albertcourt.com.sg>.* Boutique hotel with nostalgic interior décor and modern facilities. Houses a North Indian and Nepalese restaurant. Disabled access. 182 rooms.

The InnCrowd Hostel $ *73 Dunlop Street, Singapore 209401*; *tel: 6296 9169; fax: 6396 6694; <www.the-inncrowd.com>*. The InnCrowd is a basic no-frills hostel conveniently located near the Little India MRT Station. It has modest furnishings in its dorms and double rooms, broadband Internet access and a fully equipped kitchen for guests' use.

Prince of Wales $ *101 Dunlop Street, Singapore 209420; tel: 6299 0130; <www.pow.com.sg>*. An Australian-inspired backpacker hostel that's big on fun. The beer garden is a popular hangout spot; so is the pub on the first floor. Singapore and international bands play on most nights. Air-conditioned dorms and double rooms. 24 rooms.

ORCHARD ROAD

Four Seasons $$$$$ *190 Orchard Road, Singapore 248646; tel: 6734 1110; fax: 6733 0682; <www.fourseasons.com/singapore>*. Built to compete with Asia's most upscale hotels, the elegant Four Seasons has a prime location and a vast fitness and recreation centre. Disabled access. 254 rooms.

Goodwood Park $$$$ *22 Scotts Road, Singapore 228221; tel: 6737 7411; fax: 6732 8558; <www.goodwoodparkhotel.com.sg>*. A national landmark dating from 1900, this grand hotel in expansive gardens off Orchard Road is renowned for its service, fine-dining restaurants and romantic interiors. 235 rooms.

Grand Hyatt $$$$$ *10 Scotts Road, Singapore 228211; tel: 6235 4111; fax: 6734 0375; <www.singapore.grand.hyatt.com>*. A stone's throw from Orchard Road, this top luxury hotel has turned half its rooms into large business suites for business travellers. Disabled access. 663 rooms.

Hilton International $$$$ *581 Orchard Road, Singapore 238883; tel: 6737 2233; fax: 6732 2917; <www.hilton.com>*. The

Hilton has been a favourite of business travellers for its central location, rooftop pool and good dining. Disabled access. 423 rooms.

Holiday Inn Park View Singapore $$$ *11 Cavenagh Road, Singapore 229616; tel: 6733 8333; fax: 6734 4593; <www.singapore. holiday-inn.com>.* North of Orchard Road near the Istana, this Holiday Inn has clean, modern rooms, an efficient staff and a top-rated Indian restaurant. Disabled access. 315 rooms.

Marriott Hotel $$$$ *320 Orchard Road, Singapore 238865; tel: 6735 5800; fax: 6735 9800; <www.marriott.com>.* Located right at the corner of Orchard and Scotts roads, this Marriott has spacious rooms and contemporary Chinese décor inside and out. All rooms have 32-inch LCD TVs. Disabled access. 392 rooms.

Meritus Mandarin $$$$–$$$$$ *333 Orchard Road, Singapore 238867; tel: 6737 4411; fax: 6732 2361; <www.mandarin-singapore.com>.* Serious shoppers would do well to stay here as all the major malls and boutiques are within walking distance. Its 24-hour coffee house is noted for its Hainanese chicken rice. 1,200 rooms.

Orchard Hotel $$$ *442 Orchard Road, Singapore 238879; tel: 6734 7766; fax: 6733 5482; <www.orchardhotel.com.sg>.* The rooms are done up in a chic East-meets-West décor. One of Singapore's top Chinese restaurants, Hua Ting, is located here. 653 rooms.

The Regent $$$$ *1 Cuscaden Road, Singapore 249715; tel: 6733 8888; fax: 6732 8838; <www.regenthotels.com>.* Located a few blocks south of Orchard Road in the Tanglin shopping area, the Regent is a modern hotel with fairly large rooms, an airy atrium and a relaxed atmosphere. Disabled access. 439 rooms.

Shangri-La $$$$$ *22 Orange Grove Road, Singapore 258350; tel: 6737 3644; fax: 6733 1029; <www.shangri-la.com>.* For over 30 years, Shangri-La's flagship hotel in Singapore has won many international awards, deservedly so given its high level of service, spacious rooms, excellent fine dining and a commanding location in a large garden estate near Orchard Road. Disabled access. 750 rooms.

The Shatec Villa $$–$$$ *64 Lloyd Road, Singapore 239113; tel: 6734 7117; fax: 6736 1651; <www.shatec.sg>.* Several blocks south of Orchard Road, this small boutique hotel occupies a three-storey colonial mansion with Peranakan décor. 40 rooms.

Sheraton Towers $$$$ *39 Scotts Road, Singapore 228230; tel: 6737 6888; fax: 6737 1072; <www.sheraton.com/towerssingapore>.* A short walk from Orchard Road, this restful hotel is away from the bustle, yet still easily accessible. The Dining Room restaurant is especially relaxing with its cascading waterfall. 413 rooms.

Traders Hotel Singapore $$$ *1A Cuscaden Road, Singapore 249716; tel: 6738 2222; fax: 6831 4314; <www.shangri-la.com>.* Sister hotel to the upscale Shangri-La, Traders is both comfortable and practical, with excellent services and rooms, self-service laundry facilities and a large swimming pool. Disabled access. 546 rooms.

YMCA International House $$ *1 Orchard Road, Singapore 238824; tel: 6336 6000; fax: 6337 3140; <www.ymcaih.com.sg>.* A popular budget hotel, this Y has dormitories and single, twin and family rooms. There is a restaurant and a rooftop swimming pool on the premises. Requires advanced booking. 111 rooms.

SENTOSA

Costa Sands Resort $–$$ *30 Imbiah Walk, Sentosa, Singapore 099537; tel: 6275 1034; fax: 6275 1074; <www.costasands.com.sg>.* One of the budget options in Sentosa, good for groups or families who can share a rustic but air-conditioned hut (for three persons) or a chalet. A Hostelling International (HI) accommodation. 49 rooms.

Shangri-La's Rasa Sentosa Resort $$$–$$$$ *101 Siloso Road, Sentosa, Singapore 098970; tel: 6275 0100; fax: 6275 0355; <www.shangri-la.com>.* Singapore's only beachfront hotel overlooks the South China Sea. It offers a fine buffet breakfast, free watersports equipment and has a good seafood restaurant. While it is not the most convenient place to stay for access to the city, it does have a free downtown shuttle service. Disabled access. 459 rooms.

Recommended Restaurants

Singapore, with over 20,000 restaurants, cafés and food courts, has dining options to fit every taste and budget. The major cuisines are Chinese, Malay, Peranakan (a local fusion of Chinese and Malay) and Indian (both southern and northern), with healthy infusions of Indonesian, Thai and other Southeast Asian food. There are also many fine American, South American and European restaurants. Critics often hail the Asian dining in Singapore as the world's best, owing to its fresh seafood and other ingredients, its obsession with culinary matters and its position at the crossroads of Chinese, Malay and Indian dining traditions. In general, wherever one eats, from hawker centres to top international hotel restaurants, the food is likely to be first rate.

Each entry is marked with a symbol indicating the price range per person for a three-course dinner or equivalent (drinks, gratuities and taxes are not included). Lunch in the same restaurant will be less expensive than dinner.

$$$$	S$40 and more
$$$	S$20–40
$$	S$10–20
$	up to S$10

SINGAPORE RIVER

Brewerkz $$$ *01-05/06 Riverside Point, 30 Merchant Road; tel: 6438 7438; <www.brewerkz.com>*. Open daily for lunch and dinner. Handcrafted beer fresh from its on-site microbrewery and hearty American cuisine in an industrial-like setting. Brew master Scott Robertson has at least seven varieties of beer, including his best-selling India Pale Ale. Try the mussels with beer sauce.

Glutton's Bay $–$$ *01-15 Esplanade Mall; tel: 6336 7025*. Open daily for dinner. Dine on some of Singapore's best-loved street food under the moonlight. A popular spot with both locals and tourists, Glutton's Bay has 12 push-cart hawkers selling favourites like barbecued chicken wings, *char kway teow* (fried flat noodles with clams in dark sauce) and oyster omelette.

Le Saint Julien $$$$ *3 Fullerton Road, Waterboat House; tel: 6534 5947; <www.saintjulien.com.sg>.* Open Monday to Friday for lunch and dinner, Saturday for dinner only. For the best in classic comfort French cuisine, head to this elegant restaurant helmed by Julien Bompard. Do not miss the lobster bisque and soufflé. A fine wine list complements the menu.

My Humble House $$$–$$$$ *02-27/29, Esplanade Mall, 8 Raffles Avenue; tel: 6423 1881.* Open daily for lunch and dinner. Despite its name, this grand restaurant is anything but modest. Expect to be wowed by luxurious interiors and delicate Chinese dishes that come with poetic names like *Asleep in the Petals* (soft-shell crabs). Easier on the pocket are the quality local favourites with a twist from its sister outlet next door, Space@My Humble House.

Pierside Kitchen & Bar $$$–$$$$ *01-01, One Fullerton, 1 Fullerton Road; tel: 6438 0400.* Open Monday to Friday for lunch, Monday to Saturday for dinner. Chic and trendy without being intimidating, this lovely waterfront restaurant has great ambience and a modern European menu. Come for a casual lunch, a pre-theatre drink, or an intimate dinner date. The speciality is seafood, but the pretty desserts are just as big a draw. Must-haves are the oven-roasted miso cod and Valrhona chocolate fondant.

Saint Pierre $$$$ *01-01 Central Mall, 3 Magazine Road; tel: 6438 0887; <www.saintpierre.com.sg>.* Open Monday to Friday for lunch and dinner, Saturday for dinner only. One of the top spots in Singapore for high-end French cuisine given a Japanese twist. The setting is stylish, and top favourites include the innovative *foie gras* dishes, black cod in miso sauce and desserts like Grandma Stroobant's flourless chocolate cake.

Satsuma Shochu Dining Bar $$$–$$$$ *1 Nanson Road, 01-10/02-10 The Gallery Hotel; tel: 6235 3565.* Open daily for lunch and dinner. At least 20 different types of *shochu* (distilled Japanese spirit) are offered at this speciality restaurant and bar. The menu of delectable grilled skewered meats, *sashimi* and *tempura* is designed to complement the alcohol.

CIVIC DISTRICT

Doc Cheng's $$$–$$$$ *02-19 Raffles Hotel, 1 Beach Road; tel: 6431 6156.* Open Monday to Friday for lunch, daily for dinner. Doc Cheng's combines all the major Asian cuisines with the latest trends from the West to produce some real surprises.

Equinox $$$–$$$$ *68–72 Floors, Swissôtel The Stamford, 2 Stamford Road; tel: 6431 5669.* Open daily for lunch and dinner. A complex of five restaurants and bars sits atop the hotel. Start with drinks at the New Asia Bar on the 71st level while taking in stunning city views out its floor-to-ceiling windows, then descend one level to swanky French-Cambodian restaurant Jaan, decorated with Murano crystal and shimmering Cambodian silk.

Lei Garden $$$$ *01-24 CHIJMES, 30 Victoria Street; tel: 6339 3822.* Open daily for lunch and dinner. One of Singapore's best Cantonese restaurants, Lei Garden is renowned for its *dim sum* lunches and fresh seafood dishes (shark, abalone, lobster) served in an exquisite formal setting.

CHINATOWN AND CBD

Old Shanghai $$–$$$ *55 Temple Street, Chinatown; tel: 6327 1218.* Open daily for lunch and dinner. Authentic, value-for-money Shanghainese cuisine at reasonable prices. Specialities include *xiao long bao* (soup dumplings), pan-fried pork buns and drunken chicken.

Satay Street $–$$ *Lau Pa Sat, Boon Tat Street.* Open daily from 7pm. This side street is packed with street vendors serving *satay* – skewers of mutton, beef and chicken grilled over charcoal fires and served with a thick peanut gravy and *ketupat* (steamed rice cakes wrapped in coconut leaves). No credit cards.

Zhou's Kitchen $$$ *01-01 Far East Square, 7-10 Amoy Street; tel:* 6877 1123; *<www.tunglok.com>*. Open daily for lunch and dinner. For hearty Chinese fare, head to this eatery, which features alltime Chinese favourites, as well as the private recipes of the Zhou family. Dine on dishes like steamed glutinous rice with crab.

LITTLE INDIA AND KAMPONG GLAM

Banana Leaf Apolo $–$$ *54 Race Course Road, Little India; tel:* 6293 8682. Open daily. Within walking distance of Little India MRT station, this is one of the city's most popular South Indian restaurants, famed for its fiery fish-head curry. Meals are served on banana leaves. Second outlet at Little India Arcade (tel: 6297 1595).

Hajjah Maimunah $ *11–15 Jalan Pisang, Kampong Glam; tel:* 6291 3132. Open Monday to Saturday for lunch and dinner. This no-frills eatery, which serves some of the best Malay food in town, is always packed. Just point to the dishes behind the glass counter and indicate how many of you are eating. The tender beef *rendang* curry just melts in your mouth, and the *sotong bakar* (grilled squid) is exceptional. No credit cards.

Komala Vilas $–$$ *76–78 Serangoon Road, Little India; tel:* 6293 6980; *<www.komalavilas.com.sg>*. Open daily. Singapore's classic southern Indian vegetarian restaurant (six decades old) provides an unforgettable dining experience. Recommended are its spicy rice and lentil curries served on banana leaf, chutneys and *thosais* (vegetable-stuffed crêpes). Eat with your hands; wash up at sinks on the wall. Another outlet nearby at 12–14 Buffalo Road (tel: 6293 3664). No credit cards.

Tepak Sireh Restoran $$ *73 Sultan Gate, Kampong Glam; tel:* 6396 4373; *<www.tepaksireh.com.sg>*. Open daily for lunch and dinner. This resplendent mustard-coloured building next to the Istana Kampong Gelam was originally built for Malay royalty. The restaurant's recipes, reportedly handed down through generations, live up to expectations. Only buffet-style meals; recommended are its beef *rendang*, squid curry and pandan tea.

Ah Hoi's Kitchen $$–$$$ *4th Floor, Trader's Hotel, 1A Cuscaden Road; tel: 6831 4373.* Open daily for lunch and dinner. Ah Hoi's has many superb local favourites, including fried black pepper *kway teow* (rice noodles), seafood (Teochew-style prawns, fish and squid) and an unparalleled selection of stir-fried crabs in the shell, from chilli crab to pepper crab and beyond. The Ah Hoi 'pancake' is recommended for dessert.

Blu $$$$ *24th Floor, Shangri-La Hotel, 22 Orange Grove Road; tel: 6213 4598.* Open daily for dinner. With stunning city views and a swanky bar, Blu is a trendy spot to enjoy contemporary European cuisine. Excellent live jazz, wines and French champagne.

Crossroads Café $$$ *Marriott Hotel, 320 Orchard Road; tel: 6831 4605.* Open daily for breakfast, lunch and dinner. Perch yourself at this sidewalk café and watch all of Orchard Road pass by while you sample its varied and delicious mix of Singapore favourites and Asian and Western dishes.

Esmirada $$$–$$$$ *01-29 Orchard Hotel, 442 Orchard Road; tel: 6735 3476; <www.esmirada.com.sg>.* Open daily for lunch and dinner. Lively restaurant and wine bar that serves authentic hearty Mediterranean fare. Special vegetarian menus available.

House of Peranakan Cuisine $$–$$$ *Pan Pacific Orchard, 10 Claymore Road, tel: 6733 4411.* Open daily for lunch and dinner. This Straits Chinese (Peranakan) restaurant serves favourites like *sambal* (chilli) long beans and *otak-otak* (barbecued spicy fish paste), prepared from recipes that are three generations old. This restaurant also serves a fish-head curry that was once hailed by *Asian Wall Street Journal* as the best dish in Singapore.

Iggy's $$$$ *Level 3, Regent Hotel, 1 Cuscaden Road; tel: 6732 2234.* Open Monday to Friday for lunch, daily for dinner. This small, intimate modern European restaurant helmed by local culinary star Ignatius Chan has continuously won rave reviews for its innovative dishes crafted from the freshest ingredients. No à la carte, only set degustation menus. Reservations recommended.

The Line $$$–$$$$ *Shangri-La Hotel, 22 Orange Grove Road; tel: 6213 4275.* Open daily. This all-day buffet restaurant is one of the most stylish in town. The 16 culinary stations turn out freshly prepared international fare, from wood-fired pizzas to *sushi* and *dim sum*, served on Le Creuset dining ware.

Sanur $$–$$$ *04-17/18 Centrepoint, 176 Orchard Road; tel: 6734 2192.* Open daily for lunch and dinner. The excellent Indonesian and Malay dishes here include *tahu telur*, a towering beancurd and soy sauce omelet. This is also a good place for *gado gado* (Indonesian-style salad with peanut sauce) and *rojak* (fruit and vegetable salad tossed with prawn paste). Other branches are located in Ngee Ann City, Parco Bugis Junction and Suntec City.

Straits Kitchen $$$$ *Grand Hyatt Singapore, 10 Scotts Road; tel: 6732 1234.* Open daily. All of Singaporeans' favourite hawker foods are gathered at this stunning upscale restaurant. Buffet-style meals only; take your pick from the Indian, Chinese and Malay stations. Recommended are the grilled stingray and *satay*.

The Tandoor $$$–$$$$ *Basement One, Holiday Inn Park View, 11 Cavenagh Road; tel: 6730 0153.* Open daily for lunch and dinner. One of the city's most highly rated Kashmiri restaurants, the Tandoor is best known for its fresh breads and oven-baked dishes such as the lobster tandoori.

Whitebait and Kale $$$$ *01-01 Camden Medical Centre, 1 Orchard Boulevard; tel: 6333 8697.* Open daily for lunch, Mon–Sat dinner. The chefs at this Sydney-style restaurant whip up favourites like baked snapper pie and capellini (angel hair pasta) with crabmeat.

SOUTHERN SINGAPORE

Braise $$$$ *60 Palawan Beach Walk, Sentosa; tel: 6271 1929; <www.braise.com.sg>.* Open daily for lunch and dinner. This modern French restaurant sits on Palawan Beach and is ideal for a romantic night out. Recommended main courses include roasted beef with savoy cabbage, and pan-roasted seabass with sweet corn and hazelnut dressing.

The Cliff $$$–$$$$ *The Sentosa, 2 Bukit Manis Road, Sentosa; tel: 6275 0331.* Open Monday to Saturday for dinner. Perched on a cliff overlooking the South China Sea, this award-winning restaurant has all the right ingredients for a romantic dining experience. Think a beautiful sunset view, the lulling sound of lapping waves, and the freshest seafood to pamper the palate.

Il Lido $$$$ *Sentosa Golf Club, Bukit Manis Road, Sentosa; tel: 6866 1977; <www.il-lido.com>.* Open daily for lunch and dinner. Stylish and sophisticated, this fine Italian establishment is also one of the best places in Singapore to catch the sunset. Reservations required, and the dress code is smart casual.

Imperial Herbal $$$–$$$$ *1 HarbourFront Walk, 03-08 Vivo-City; tel: 6337 0491.* Open daily for lunch and dinner. This traditional Chinese restaurant, formerly located at the Metropole Hotel, is well known for its tasty health-boosting soups devised to restore your internal *yin* and *yang* balance.

HOLLAND VILLAGE AND SURROUNDS

Bunalun $$–$$$ *3 Jalan Merah Saga, 01-70 Chip Bee Gardens, tel: 6472 0870; <www.bunalun.com.sg>.* Open daily. A chic, breezy organic café that dishes up delicious gourmet meals and ready-to-go salads, crab cakes and pastries. The retail section stocks a good range of organic produce as well as home and beauty products under the Bunalun label.

Graze $$$–$$$$ *4 Rochester Park; tel: 6775 9000; <www.graze.sg>.* Open Tuesday to Sunday for dinner, Sunday for breakfast, brunch and lunch. Owned by the same people behind the hip JIA boutique hotels, this stylish restaurant is housed in a beautiful pre-war, black-and-white house in Rochester Park, the city's hip new dining hub. The cuisine is modern Western–Asian cuisine, and at weekends, a hearty breakfast and brunch is also served. After dinner you can chill out in its lounge bar, Mint, with an outdoor terrace. Also has a gourmet-produce shop and an outdoor cinema.

Original Sin $$–$$$ *Block 43 Jalan Merah Saga, 01-62 Chip Bee Gardens; tel: 6475 5605; <www.originalsin.com.sg>.* Open Tuesday to Sunday for lunch, daily for dinner. This vegetarian restaurant specialises in Italian and Mediterranean fare, with knockout mock-meat cannelloni and pizzas as well as superb risotto, pasta and salads, in a European setting.

EAST COAST

Kim Choo $$ *109 East Coast Road; tel: 6440 5590.* Open daily for lunch and dinner. This two-storey restaurant is known for its simple home-cooked Peranakan food. Order the *assam* fish head cooked with tomato, pineapple and okra, classic *bangwan kepiting* (soup with crabmeat and pinced pork balls) and *babi pongteh* (stewed pork with fermented beans, bamboo shoots and mushrooms). Kim Choo is also famous for its glutinous rice dumplings and you can sign up for a class in making these.

Red House Seafood $$–$$$ *Block 1204 East Coast Parkway, 01-05; tel: 6442 3112; <www.redhouseseafood.com>.* Open daily for dinner, Saturday, Sunday and public holidays for lunch. There are a dozen good seafood restaurants at the East Coast Seafood Centre along the East Coast Parkway. Red House is one of the best and most crowded (no reservations), offering informal outdoor seafood dining. Dishes like chilli crab and drunken prawns are always fresh and superbly prepared.

Vansh $$–$$$$ *01-04 Singapore Indoor Stadium, 2 Stadium Walk; tel: 6345 4466; <www.vansh.com.sg>.* Open daily for lunch and dinner. Offering fine examples of New Asian cuisine, this restaurant near the Kallang River combines a groovy, intimate ambience with modern Indian dishes. On the menu is a range of tapas, tandoori and teppan-style meals.

INDEX

Abdul Gafoor
Mosque 50
Al-Abrar Mosque 49
Ann Siang Road 46
Arab Street 54
Armenian Church 34
Arts House, The 26
Asian Civilisations
Museum, Armenian
Street 34
Asian Civilisations
Museum, Empress
Place 25

Battle Box 36
Boat Quay 29–30, 90
Bugis Street 57
Bukit Timah Nature
Reserve 67, 94

Cathedral of the
Good Shepherd 39
Cavenagh Bridge 27
Central Business
District 27
CHIJMES 38, 91
Chinatown 41, 85
Chinatown Heritage
Centre 42
Chinatown Night
Market 44
Chinatown Food Street 44
Chinese Garden 63
City Hall 31, 33
Clarke Quay 30
Club Street 47

East Coast Park 93
Emerald Hill 59, 92
Empress Place
Waterfront 26

Esplanade – Theatres on
the Bay 28, 90

Far East Square 48
Fort Canning Park 35
Fullerton Hotel 27
Fuk Tak Chi Musuem 48

Geylang Serai 61
Goodwood Park Hotel 60

Haji Lane 56
Hajjah Fatimah
Mosque 56
HarbourFront Centre 86
Haw Par Villa (Tiger
Balm Gardens) 64, 96
Hotel 1926 46
Hua Song Museum 65

Istana 60
Istana Kampong
Gelam 55

Jamae Mosque 42
Japanese Garden 63
Jinriksha Station 45
Jurong BirdPark 66, 96

Kampong Glam 54
Katong 61
Keong Saik Road 46
Kusu Island 77
Kwan Im Thong Hood
Cho Temple 58

Lau Pa Sat 99
Lee Kuan Yew 19
Leong San Buddhist
Temple 53
Little India 50, 86

MacRitchie Reservoir
Park 68
Malabar Jamaath
Mosque 56
Malay Village 61
Malay Heritage Centre 55
Mandai Orchid
Gardens 69
Marina Bay 29
Maxwell Food Centre
46, 99
Merlion Park 27
Mint Museum of
Toys 40
Museum of Shanghai
Toys 52
Mustafa Centre 52, 86

Nagore Durgha Shrine 48
National Library 57
National Museum 37
National Orchid
Garden 63
Newton Circus food
centre 99
Night Safari 71, 96

One Fullerton 27
Orchard Road 59, 84, 92

Padang 33
Pulau Ubin 78

Raffles Hotel 39
Raffles Hotel Museum
26, 40
Raffles' Landing Site 25
Raffles Place 27
red dot design
museum 49
Robertson Quay 30

St Andrew's Cathedral 31
St John's Island 77
Sakya Muni Buddha
    Gaya Temple 53
Sculpture Square 58
Sentosa 73, 93, 96
Singapore Art Museum 37
Singapore Botanic
    Gardens 62
Singapore City Gallery 46
Singapore Cricket
    Club 34
Singapore Discovery
    Centre 96
Singapore Repertory
    Theatre 31
Singapore River 27, 90

Singapore Science
    Centre 96
Singapore Tyler
    Print Institute 31
Singapore Zoo 69, 96
Snow City 96
Sri Krishnan Temple 58
Sri Mariamman Temple 43
Sri Srinivasa
    Perumal Temple 52
Sri Veeramakaliamman
    Temple 51
Substation, The 35
Sultan Mosque 55
Sungei Buloh
    Wetland Reserve 94
Suntec City 29, 82

Supreme Court 33

Tanjong Pagar
    Conservation
    District 46
Tekka Centre 50, 86
Telok Ayer Chinese
    Methodist Church 49
Telok Ayer Street 48
Thian Hock Keng
    Temple 49

Victoria Theatre and
    Concert Hall 26
VivoCity 73, 86

Waterloo Street 58

Berlitz pocket guide

Singapore

Fifth Edition 2008
Reprinted 2009

Written by J.D. Brown and Margaret Backenheimer
Updated by Wyn-Lyn Tan
Edited by Low Jat Leng
Managing Editor: Francis Dorai
Series Editor: Tony Halliday

Printed in Singapore by Insight Print
Services (Pte) Ltd, 38 Joo Koon Road,
Singapore 628990. Tel: (65) 6865-1600.
Fax: (65) 6861-6438

Berlitz Trademark Reg. U.S. Patent Office
and other countries. Marca Registrada

Photography credits
All photography by Jack Hollingsworth/APA
except for Alain Compost 68; Alain Evrard/Bes
Stock 24, 26; APA Photo Agency 34; CHIJMES 91;
Corbis 20; Denise Tackett/APA 79; Derrick Lim/
APA 22; Escape Theme Park 96; Far East
Organization 48; iStockphoto 44; Javad Namazie
57; Jonathan Koh/APA 6, 9, 13, 29, 30, 43, 49, 59,
65, 85, 86, 94, 99, 100, 107; John Lamb/Stone/
Getty Images 39; Mary Evans 15, 16, 17; National
Museum of Singapore 3TR, 37; National Orchid
Garden 63; Night Safari 3CL; Raffles Hotel 2B, 40;
Sentosa 3CR, 73, 74, 75, 76, 95; Singapore Art
Museum 38; Swissôtel The Stamford 92; Tony
Ying/APA 10, 33, 41; Topham 18
Cover picture: Justin Guariglia/Corbis

Every effort has been made to provide
accurate information in this publication,
but changes are inevitable. The publisher
cannot be responsible for any resulting
loss, inconvenience or injury.

Contact us

At Berlitz we strive to keep our guides as
accurate and up to date as possible, but if you
find anything that has changed, or if you have
any suggestions on ways to improve this guide,
then we would be delighted to hear from you.

Berlitz Publishing, PO Box 7910,
London SE1 1WE, England.
fax: (44) 20 7403 0290
email: berlitz@apaguide.co.uk
www.berlitzpublishing.com